T0366161

APPROACHING POSTCOLONIAL AND PSYCHOANALYTIC CRITICISM IN LITERARY STUDIES:
AN ILLUSTRATION OF AN ANALYSIS OF A MALAYSIAN NOVEL

SUBARNA SIVAPALAN

PARTRIDGE

A Penguin Random House Company

To order additional copies of this book, contact
Toll Free 800 101 2657 (Singapore)
Toll Free 1 800 81 7340 (Malaysia)
orders.singapore@partridgepublishing.com

www.partridgepublishing.com/singapore

ACKNOWLEDGEMENT

I would like to dedicate this book to Dr Ganakumaran Subramaniam, the President of the Malaysian English Language Teaching Association (MELTA) for instilling in me the passion and perseverance to take up the study on which this book has been based on. I am most thankful to him for supervising this study, and patiently reading through and approving every single word written. The birth of this book would not have been possible without his guidance.

This book is also dedicated to all undergraduate and postgraduate students aspiring to take on the challenges of research within the area of Language and Literary analysis. May your literary research journey be a fulfilling one.

To my parents, husband, sister and daughter, Yuvena, thank you so much for your support and patience.

PREFACE

This book is a contribution to the growing body of work on language and literary studies in Malaysia. The book encompasses the analysis of a common theme found in many Malaysian novels, i.e. identity and sense of self. These themes are examined through postcolonial and psychoanalytical lenses. The book provides an illustration of the intricacies that go into literary analysis, namely in the manner in which literary research and analysis is conceptualized and carried out. As such, the book has been written in a format that reflects the way in which a literary analysis of a text is conducted. It is hoped that this book will provide Language and Literature undergraduate and postgraduate students with guidance on the manner in which literary and textual analysis of literary texts could be approached.

Appeals to the past are among the commonest of strategies in interpretations of the present. What animates such appeals is not only disagreement about what happened in the past and what the past was, but uncertainty about whether the past really is past, over and concluded, or whether it continues, albeit in different forms, perhaps.

(Said 1979: 85)

INTRODUCTION

INTRODUCTION

> London, the lost city of Atlantis, under an ocean of fog; and I am one of its denizens, groping, and groping towards the pin-point punctures of the lamps opposite. Out from the misty closeness swam the dark ghouls in overcoats and hats—the limbs moving stiffly as if fighting their way against some treacherous currents.

> (Lee Kok Liang, 1952)

This study is an analysis of the semi-autobiographical novel, *London Does Not Belong to Me* (LDNBTM), written by the legendary Malaysian Chinese writer Lee Kok Liang (1927-1992). Lee Kok Liang began LDNBTM on board a passenger ship, which took him back from England to Malaya in 1954. Published only in 2003, 11 years after his demise, the author's first novel was enthused by his own experiences in London while he completed his law degree at Lincoln's Inn.

LDNBTM is a postcolonial Malaysian novel which deals with the concept of transculturation in postcolonial individuals. Transculturation is a term which is used in postcolonial theory to refer to the manner in which subordinated or marginalized groups select and invent from materials transmitted to them by a dominant culture (Ashcroft, Griffiths & Tiffin 1998). The process of migration is a possible foundation of transculturation. The migratory process, which is often undertaken for the purpose of survival, education or career enhancement, leads these migrant individuals to experiment with the culture of this new society (host society) they come into contact with (Tajfel 1982). This contact produces transcultural tendencies in the individual.

However it must be emphasised at this point that not all transcultural tendencies are produced from the willingness of individuals to assimilate with the host society. These 'transcultural productions, which are often projected through postcolonial undertones, result in a changed identity in the individual, creating new cultural experiences for these individuals (Tajfel & Turner 1986). These experiences differ from the experiences they encounter in their homeland' (Sivapalan, 2007: 125).

This study will analyse the postcolonial individual's search for identity and sense of self. Transcultural experiences of the protagonist were chosen over cross-cultural and intercultural experiences as transculturalism deals with the form of culture created not from within separate spheres, but in the holistic forms of diverse cultures. This form was also chosen based on the principle that a single culture, in and of itself, is incomplete and requires interaction and dialogue with other cultures. The intent of this study is also to investigate the effects of transcultural experiences on the protagonist's identity and sense of self. The protagonist's search for identity and sense of self will be analysed using psychoanalysis and the postcolonial theory.

NEGOTIATING IDENTITY

Transcultural circumstances allow the individual to select and invent from the culture of the new society they associate themselves with. According to Pratt (1992), the process of transcultural negotiation can cast the identity of the individual in a new light. This is because transcultural experiences can influence and affect the individual's sense of self and identity of their homeland as well as alter it in the country they migrate to (Pratt 1992). As a result of these transcultural experiences, the individual could assimilate, reject or fight against the culture of the new society and the culture of his homeland.

The assimilating, rejecting or fighting phase is related closely to Frantz Fanon's views of the postcolonial writer's negotiation of identity. Fanon's evolutionary schema advances three phases. These phases are the assimilation phase, the cultural nationalist phase and the nationalist phase. In the phase of assimilation, the 'native intellectual gives proof that he has assimilated the culture of the occupying power' (Fanon 1966: 178). The literary productions of the native at this phase bears resemblance to the literary traditions of the colonizing country. The native's incorporation of the colonial context is projected and produced in his works. The second phase sees the native intellectual in recollection of his genuine identity. It is in this stage that the native resists endeavours to assimilate him. However, owing to his own cultural isolation, the native intellectual's attempt at cultural reaffirmation 'stop at romanticization of bygone days corrected by philosophical traditions and aesthetic conventions borrowed from the world of the colonizer' (Amuta 1989). The nationalist phase is the phase in which the native man of culture 'after having tried to lose himself in the people and with the people, will on the contrary shake the people' (Fanon 1966 :179). This phase, according to Fanon, is also known as the fighting phase. In this phase, the revolutionary and nationalist phase in the literature of the colonized is seen, in which the exposure of more natives to the realities to a democratization of the force of literary expression is witnessed (Fanon 1966). According to Fanon, during this phase, many natives who would never have thought of producing literary work begin to feel the need to express themselves. The inclusion of Fanon's evolutionary scheme is vital to the comprehension of the characters in the novel. This scheme is especially useful in the deciphering of the speech, thoughts and actions of the expatriate individuals in Lee Kok Liang's work. It also promotes an enhanced comprehension of Lee Kok Liang's own feelings regarding his identity as a postcolonial individual and writer.

The protagonist in LDNBTM faces a situation comparable to that described by Fanon. The protagonist is an immigrant Chinese Malaysian who migrates to Britain for a couple of years in pursue of education. Upon his arrival in Britain, the protagonist who seems to be rather westernised realises the need to select and invent from the culture of the host society (British society). The encounter he experiences compels him to negotiate his identity between memories of his Malayan homeland and the modifications to his identity under transcultural circumstances he experiences in London. This research therefore sees the need to explore the journey taken by the protagonist in the process of negotiating and reconciling his Malaysian Chinese immigrant identity with the modifications to his identity under transcultural conditions in London. This study will examine if the protagonist's negotiation of identity is done in a conscious manner or is carried out unconsciously. It will examine what happens to the postcolonial individual who is in contact with transcultural experiences and the manner in which these experiences affect his identity and sense of self. This research will also attempt to identify if his transcultural experience in London prepares him to deal better with the environment when he returns to Malaya or leaves him feeling confused and lost.

As the analysis involves the need to examine the feelings, emotions and relationships of the protagonist and the characters he comes into contact with, the use of psychoanalysis is seen to be an important tool to the research. As feelings, emotions and relationships cannot be studied superficially, psychology related models are useful in the comprehension of the feelings, thoughts and relationships of the characters. Postcolonial theory will also be employed in the analysis of the protagonist's identity and sense of self. Postcolonial theory is useful in deciphering the relationship between the individual and society. Postcolonial theory is valuable to the research as it would be useful in examining the manner in which the protagonist is treated by his homeland society and the British society.

THE LIFE AND WORK
OF LEE KOK LIANG

LEE KOK LIANG-A BRIEF LIFE HISTORY OF THE WRITER

The focus of this book is the novel *London Does Not Belong to Me* by Lee Kok Liang, who is incidentally one of Malaysia's most prominent literary figures whose works in English have earned him significant commendation nationally as well as internationally. Starting out as a fiction writer, Lee developed his skills during the colonial period in British Malaya. Lee was considered the first mature Malayan writer writing in English. Thus, this section will comprise a discussion on the life and works of the novelist. It is hoped that the information provided here will aid readers understand Lee Kok Liang's approach.

Lee Kok Liang was born in Alor Setar, Kedah in 1927, and is of Hokkien Chinese descent. He received his education in an English school. However, during the Japanese occupation, his education was in Chinese, because the Japanese stopped the teaching of English. In 1949, he went to Melbourne University to pursue a degree in Arts and Law. He then went on to complete his legal studies at the Inns of Court. Upon his return to Malaya, he was called to the Bar in Penang in 1954. For a period, Lee Kok Liang was active in local politics. He was a member of the Socialist Front and was also elected to the Penang Municipal Council between the years 1958-1963. He was also appointed to the State Assembly from 1959-1964 after winning the Tanjung State Assembly seat (Fadillah Merican et al. 2004). John Barnes (1985) in his article *The Fiction of Lee Kok Liang* states that the writer's political activities and professional activities limited the time he could give to his writing. Even so, Lee managed to juggle his zeal for writing, his law vocation and his marriage outstandingly well.

He began serious fiction writing in Melbourne University, while pursuing his studies there. 'Part of the stimulus came from a course in modern English literature. He was delighted to discover that one of his fellow students was a granddaughter of Rider Haggard, the author whom he had devoured in his boyhood' (Barnes 1985: 185). During his years in the university, Lee read English and Continental fiction. These readings were an integral part of his experiences, which later paved the way to his writing debut. Lee wrote in the English language. His subjects were drawn mostly from the immigrant Chinese community, of which he was a part of (Fadillah Merican et al. 2004). Commenting on his language preferences, Lee said,

> In our early teens, we were confronted with fear and tension. Each of us sought an escape in our own ways. For me, it meant reading voraciously tales of warfare and generals-the classics of the opera, Cantonese and Hokkien. I did not feel at all strange dropping a book in Chinese and picking one up in English; it was a period when language did not have any sociological tinge or stance. And it never crossed my mind whether my English overlapped my Chinese or my Chinese overpowered my English. I did not feel strongly, nor did anyone worry or fuss, about what my language was.
>
> (1985: 51)

In an interview conducted by Lim Ai Lee which was published in the New Straits Times, Lee Kok Liang commented that the characters in his fiction are partly based upon real figures, people whom he had met sometime or other in his life. Lee says that 'You cannot completely shut off real life in fiction. The characters in my short story or novels could be based on real people who through a process of imaginative reconstruction, are fictionalised and used to put my view of the world across' (1992: 34).

Harrex (1982) in his paper *Scalpel, Scar, Icon: Lee Kok Liang's Flowers in the Sky* notes that Lee's characters, however morbid their destiny may be, strike as 'sketches and familiars' imitative of life. According to Woods (1990), Lee's characters are also drawn firmly from the inferior and middle class, instead of being given any suggestion of classical heroism or Romantic escapism. The physical settings of his works are drawn mostly within the vicinities of Penang and Ipoh (Harrex 1982). His favourite themes include issues on identity, sense of belonging and alienation. Lee's fiction 'does not lie in documentation but in its revelation of the inner characteristics of Malaysian life' (Barnes 1985: 185). Barnes adds that his fascinations also lie within what is profoundly human.

Lee's first written story was published in 1949 in the journal *Present Opinion*. This journal was issued by the Melbourne University Arts Association. In 1950 and 1951, he wrote *The Pei-Pa* and *Ami to Fu*. These writings appeared in the Melbourne University magazine, of which he was co-editor (the 1951 issue), making him the only Asian editor to make it to the list of Melbourne University magazine editors list from the years 1901-1981. The stories that appeared in 1950 and 1951 are evidences of his maturing art and revealed how early he had found his own voice (Barnes 1985). By the time Lee published *The Mutes in the Sun* in 1964, he had been an accomplished writer of stories in English. In early 1964, T. S. Wignesan singled him out as one of the best writers of English fiction in the country. Sharilyn Woods (1990), in her article, *Silence, Communication and Cultural Conflict in Lee Kok Liang's 'The Mutes in the Sun' and 'Flowers in the Sky'*, states that Lee's artistic accomplishments included a precise use of regional details or local colour, a narrative method which created an exciting sense of realism, and a determined portrayal of character described as naturalism. *Return to Malaya* which forms part of the final section of *The Mutes in the Sun* has been praised for its use of minute details. These details, says Woods, are 'illustrated from the perceptible and blatant world of British Malaya, more accurately in Penang, where Lee spent his seminal years' (1990: 191).

Apart from writing, Lee Kok Liang has also contributed to the development of Malaysian literature in English. He was the editorial consultant of *Tenggara* from 1967 to 1969. He was also elected to judge the New Straits Times Short Story competition from 1987 to 1992 (Fadillah Merican et al. 2004). Lee Kok Liang was in his own way a revolutionist writer. Lee Kok Liang did not theorize but weaved his thoughts and ideas into his fiction. His latest novel, *London Does Not Belong to Me*, 'carries a loaded historical perspective. It explores the possibilities of association with or disassociation from the colonial culture' that initiated writing in English in Malaysia (Maniam 2003: 3).

When Lee Kok Liang handed over a manuscript to Syd Harrex at the Singapore Writers' Week in 1986, neither of them envisioned that Lee's first, unpublished novel would appear posthumously (Harrex 2003). Harrex co-edited the novel *London Does Not Belong to Me* with his one-time PhD student, Bernard Wilson. Its recent publication comes more than a decade after Lee's sudden death in 1992. *London Does Not Belong to Me* was begun by Lee Kok Liang on board a passenger ship as it took him back to Malaya from England in 1954. The book was motivated by the author's own experiences in London while he finished his law degree at Lincoln's Inn. The book, according to Harrex, is an early example of a literary work that deals with issues of being displaced and alienated from English culture, and in many ways it anticipates the modern genre known as post-colonial literature (Harrex: 2003).

Lee Kok Liang's demise on the eve of Christmas in the year 1992 came as a shock to many. At the time of his death, Lee was in the midst of completing his novel tentatively titled *The Magical Moments of Mollika*. This was his third compilation of short stories. He was also working on the book *Fairy Tales for God Daughters* of which the story *Ah Tong and the Horseface Princess* was a feature. Alike the novel *London Does Not Belong to Me*, *The Magical Moments of Mollika* was also published posthumously (Fadillah Merican et al. 2004).

INFLUENCES, TECHNIQUES AND ISSUES IN THE WORKS OF LEE KOK LIANG

Criticism on the works of Lee Kok Liang can be found but not in great quantity. However, in this section, I will not delve into a meticulous account of each of his works. Instead, selective criticism of selected short stories and the novel *London Does Not Belong to Me* will be dealt with in a very brief manner. These criticisms will encompass the influences, techniques and the issues he brings across through his works. Criticism of Lee's works are rather important to this study as it helps with the comprehension of the feelings and relationships of the characters portrayed in his works, particularly in *London Does Not Belong To Me*.

Lee Kok Liang drew much of his inspiration from the immigrant Chinese community he belonged to. The early immigration period saw the Chinese community being communal and clustered together in respective clans. As such, each clan member would be very dependent on other members. According to Lee Kok Liang, this social environment makes one look closely at others within the community. Lee Kok Liang drew the ideas of his early works from this very kind of scenario. He adds that most of his works were based upon personal and social experiences derived from childhood and everything that went around him. In his own words, Lee Kok Liang admitted that the only influence on his works were his experiences and the things that happened around him. Lee Kok Liang wrote because he wanted to write and also because he hoped to captivate the hearts of his readers (Fadillah Merican et al. 2004).

In addition to the immigrant Chinese of Malaysia, another of his greatest influence was Anton Chekhov. Lee Kok Liang's fascination with the writer Chekhov was due to his (Chekhov's) philosophy of freedom of expression. He was also fascinated with the works of Rider Haggard (Barnes 1985). Although Lee Kok Liang has numerous times stressed that his law career had no influence whatsoever over his writing methods, his fiction often draw upon themes of justice and fair play.

Lee Kok Liang's novels are also influenced by the scenes of ordinary or everyday life and people. These scenes were usually based upon his own experiences and what he noticed around him. His novels and short stories were often set around Penang and Ipoh and the Chinese community. Fadillah Merican et al. (2004), echoing similar views to that of Wood states that Lee Kok Liang's depiction of the people of lower class are often seen in his portrayal of the poor and the physically handicapped, for instance his depiction of the mutes in *Mutes in the Sun* and *Flowers in the Sky*.

According to Fadillah Merican et al. (2004), Lee Kok Liang's novels can also be categorised as truly Malaysian. This is due to the fact that his novels often include influences of local colour in the speech, setting, social structure and customs. Lee Kok Liang's depictions are of Penang in particular and Malaysia in general. John Barnes (1985), in his article titled *The Fiction of Lee Kok Liang* asserts that the appeal of Lee's fiction does not lie in documentation but in its revelation of the inner characteristics of Malaysian life. Barnes is of the opinion that 'at documentary level it is certainly authentic-or at least, it feels authentic to the outsider in its delicately exact observation of everyday living-but its purposes go far beyond the mere description of appearances' (1985: 185). Lee Kok Liang's concern, continues Barnes, lies primarily with the profound being more closely rather than with local colour. Kirpal Singh in *Transcending Context: The World of Lee Kok Liang's Fiction* agrees also to the fact that the fiction of the author is drawn from the 'pluralistic society of Malaysia' (2000:205). Kirpal (1981) believes that Lee Kok Liang writes best when he uses an unpretentious and ironic tone in describing situations he knows well. Harrex (1982) on the other hand observes that Lee Kok Liang's affinity is with a modernism that derives from Kafka rather than Zola. Harrex continues that the author's fiction 'uncover, beneath the documented surfaces of experience, not so much adducible cause and effect as a sense of peril, horror and awe induced by the grotesque and mysterious in human nature' (1982: 174). Fadillah Merican et al. (2004) notes that Lee Kok Liang's themes have a certain control over the presentation of his characters. Harrex (1982) adds that Lee Kok Liang's perception of cultural setting is also individualistic.

The theme of human failure to communicate pervades most of Lee Kok Liang's works. This is depicted by Lee Kok Liang through his mute characters. Another favourite theme Lee Kok Liang portrays in his fiction is the theme of displacement and alienation. In *Scalpel, Scar, Icon: Lee Kok Liang's Flower's in the Sky,* the author is of the opinion that Lee's characters are alienated, ostracised victims of a deformed world out of their own control (Harrex 1982: 174). The consciousness of personal imperfection is also a common subject matter of most of his writings. This imperfection is dealt with more comprehensively with psychosomatic keenness. The individual's search for identity is another common feature of his works like *London Does Not Belong to Me* and *Ibrahim Something.* Kwan Terry (1984) represents Lee Kok Liang's fascination with the theme of identity rather accurately. Kwan Terry observes that Lee Kok Liang's stories 'identify features which point to a character's inner agitation that colours his moral impetus towards judgement to changed realities.' However, 'this inner agitation does not form part of the character's conscious life and which suggests a submerged conflict in the roots of the character's personality' (Kwan-Terry 1984).

Each writer has a trademark technique of their own. As, such, Lee Kok Liang's writings are also based upon several techniques. Among these techniques include the concept of interior monologue and flashbacks. More often than not, the author's stories also end without a conclusion. This technique employed by Lee Kok Liang is what Harrex (1982) identifies as the technique of 'restricted focus or incomplete vision'. Abdul Majid Nabi Baksh (1984) in his paper *Theme and Technique in Lee Kok Liang's Flowers in the Sky* is of the view that the author uses the technique of restricted focus to captivate and maintain the attention of the reader. With regards to the author's use of the technique of flashbacks, this technique is used to create a sense of sympathy towards the characters of his fiction. In addition to evoking the reader's sense of sympathy, the flashback technique also helps make Lee Kok Liang's characters appear more human. The use of this technique also assists the author in his portrayal of transitory movements from the present to the past in his fiction (Fadillah Merican et al. 2004). Lee Kok Liang's use of the interior monologue technique, notes Fadillah Merican et al. (2004) is manoeuvred through the minds of his characters. Lee Kok Liang's use of this technique is aptly discussed by Abdul Majid Nabi Baksh. According to Abdul Majid (1984), the author's narrative technique is seen at play through two distinct frames.

> First, there is the action in the here and now, in the objective or external world, which is usually but not always the immediate present of the novel. This can be termed the objective frame. Co-existing with the frame provided by the action in the objective world is an internal frame consisting of interior monologues through which the characters reveal the impact on them, the action in the objective world and of associated events . . . The transition from the objective frame or world to the interior monologue, into the mind of the character, is smoothly and naturally affected by the association of ideas . . . The association of ideas is used not only to

move from the objective to the internal world but also from the internal monologue to the objective world.

(Abdul Majid bin Baksh 1984: 16)

In the introduction to the novel *London Does Not Belong to Me*, K. S. Maniam observes that the author uses the technique of witnessing in his narration of the novel. Maniam notes that throughout the novel, the characters 'watch each other, lie in wait for each other, they observe each other, attempt to penetrate-in more ways than one-each other and, finally move away from being inhibited by the other'(2003: 3). This is best seen in the character of the protagonist.

Wong Phui Nam, a prominent literary figure in Malaysia has much praise for Lee Kok Liang's narration. Wong comments,

> It is not very often that we come across a writer who can take us below the surface of our conscious everyday lives to a direct perception of the instinctual drives that feed our motives and those actions that ultimately bring back to us intense psychological suffering and so show us something of our mortal condition of which not only the Buddha but other spiritual masters down the age have spoken. Among Malaysian writers, Lee Kok Liang alone, so far, has shown that capacity. There is in his writing, an imaginative realisation of thought as it is being formed and translated into action in ordinary people caught in stressful relationships. His realisation is so intense that in reading his works, we gain a sense of power of the instinctual forces that move people. Through the writing we have a sense of the suffering that attends upon all lives touched by the fires fed from these forces.

(1992:33)

Lee Kok Liang's narrative excellence is seen in his ability to provide clear and accurate descriptions of events. His experiences coupled with his creative genius on subject matters familiar to him give him the ability to 'allow realistic presentations' of the events (Fadillah Merican et al. 2004). Critic Harrex (1982) observes that Lee Kok Liang's narrative preserves Malaysian flavours, tones and textures to create a sense of contemporary to represent Malaysian time, place and setting. In his paper titled *Narration and the Structure of Experience: The Fiction of Lee Kok Liang*, John Kwan-Terry (1984) acknowledges the author's ability to provide visual force in explicating sentiment in concrete imagery through localized background which has public significance. Wood in her reading of Ee Tiang Hong's criticism on *The Mutes in the Sun* says that Lee Kok Liang is among the few who have attempted with any success to portray the linguistic and cultural diversity in Malaysia, who have something to say about the human condition, and who say it with more than passing interest' (1990: 193). Kirpal Singh commenting on Lee Kok Liang's works is of the belief that Lee's depiction of psychic displacement within a pluralistic context is illustrated powerfully by individual characters whose own natures and actions suggest an over-riding destiny against which they seem powerless (2000: 204). According to Fadillah Merican et al. (2004), Lee Kok Liang's works are sketches of social responsiveness in a multi-racial nation.

The essence of Lee Kok Liang's fiction also lies in his ability to portray sound descriptions of characters. Wood (1990) likens Lee's characters to common men and women of the European Realistic tradition. Wood observes that Lee Kok Liang's characters are among the dispossessed of the society, for instance, the homeless, the poor, the ill, the uneducated and a host of individuals who are without hope, without direction and are voiceless. These characters are likened to the 'mutes of the city' and as a single entity, they form the deformed individuals of the society. Commenting on Lee Kok Liang's characters, Kwan-Terry (1984) notes that Lee Kok Liang's characters are shaped by forces the characters cannot control. These forces include the layers of the character's nature, the cultural habits of the characters, social habits and 'circumstances and environment that form an imprisoning world with man located in the centre'. It is thus both man's fate and estate that without these imprisoning layers, he is indefinable' (Kwan-Terry 1984). These in turn leads him on a journey of self-discovery and the seeking of a true identity. In the process of negotiating their crisis of identity, Lee Kok Liang's characters are often faced with the predicament of alienation, displacement and a lost sense of belonging. In order to highlight the predicament of alienated and displaced characters, Fadillah Merican et al. (2004) remarks that Lee Kok Liang depicts his characters with an ironic twist. He cites the example of Ah Lan, the mute girl in *Flowers in the Sky* who is portrayed as a temptress to heighten the sexual consciousness of the monk.

The theme of identity crisis is depicted in his latest novel *London Does Not Belong to Me*. According to Bernard Wilson (2003), *London Does Not Belong to Me* deals with the disillusion and isolation of marginalized people as shown through a contrasting collection of expatriates who seek to establish identity, purpose and a sense of belonging in an alien environment. Lee also attempts at an exploration of self in the context of an environment that is both familiar to the author and narrator. Syd Harrex is also of a similar view. Harrex (2003) believes that the book is an early example of a literary work that deals with issues of being displaced and alienated from English culture. Fadillah Merican et al. (2004) points further that the conflicts faced by the characters in his writings are resulted by external and internal changes as well as efforts to come to terms with unfulfilled wishes. The novel is also a traditional novel dealing with personal relationships, at the emotional, psychological and cultural level. At the same time, the novel is also an innovative fiction which brings into interrelated focus the marginalisation in London of two subcultures, i.e. the expatriate colonials and the gay community. There is also a sense of loss and rejection at a personal level, which is reinforced and complemented by what is happening in the social situation. (Harrex 2003). In the novel, the author also does not seem to place much emphasis on the names of his characters. In *London Does Not Belong to Me* for instance, the characters can only be identified by their first names. The protagonist in the novel is also left nameless.

Lee Kok Liang's contributions to Malaysia and Malaysian literature in English are of immense importance and significance. Citing Kee Thuan Chye, Fadillah Merican et al. (2004) makes clear that Lee Kok Liang's works are significant deliveries of lifestyle, systems of values, thinking and customs that are changing with time. He had also been dubbed as one of the foremost writers in English fiction as early as 1968, when the corpus of Malaysian literature in English was still at its conception stage. His 30 years of experience is proof of his literary expertise. Many Malaysian writers and academics in the English language, to this very day, consider Lee Kok Liang the 'guru' of Malaysian literature in English. Among them include K. S. Maniam, Wong Phui Nam, Lloyd Fernando, T. Wignesan and Kee Thuan Chye.

THEORETICAL BACKGROUND & METHODOLOGY

INTRODUCTION

This chapter will deal with the theories as well as the methodology employed in the research. As this study investigates the concept of identity and sense of self in transcultural experiences, the theories that will be most functional in the examination of the notion of identity and sense of self are the postcolonial theory and the theory of psychoanalysis. The study will focus on the analytical psychology approach of the psychoanalysis theory. This theory focuses upon the formation and development of the human identity and psyche in relation to feelings and relationships based upon the individual's speech, thoughts and action. Hence, knowledge of the analytical psychology approach will be useful in the examination of the psyche of the character of the protagonist in LDNBTM.

Postcolonial theory is helpful in the comprehension of the identity of the postcolonial individual as it helps analyse the position and function of the individual in society. This theory also gives the study a strong analytical base of important concepts like transculturation, alienation, otherness, displacement, marginalization, identity and sense of belonging. These concepts are essential in the analysis of the postcolonial individual's search for his identity and sense of self in a transcultural context. This theory will be applied upon the characterization of the protagonist in LDNBTM to assist in the assessment of his evolving sense of self, as a result of transcultural experiences in London and Malaya. The analysis of the notion of identity will also be completed by also using the social identity theory. Social identity theory is a branch of the theory of sociology. The focus of this theory is on the importance of social identity as a factor in the individual's sense of self-identity. This theory has been chosen as it links closely with the psychological make-up of the individual. The social identity theory that has been employed for the purpose of this research is that of Tajfel and Turner's (1986).

THE POSTCOLONIAL INDIVIDUAL AND HIS NEGOTIATION OF IDENTITY

Since LDNBTM is a postcolonial novel, it is necessary to first provide readers with a brief overview of the postcolonial situation. Knowledge of the postcolonial situation would assist readers in understanding the character and psyche of the protagonist. The field of Postcolonial studies has been gaining prominence since the 1970s. Some academics date its rise in the West, owing it to Edward Said's significant critique of Western constructions and interpretations of the Orient in his book, *Orientalism*. The growing importance of the term 'postcolonial' was strengthened by the publication of *The Empire Writes Back: Theory and Practice in Post-Colonial Literatures* by Bill Ashcroft, Gareth Griffiths, and Helen Tiffin in the year 1989.

Although there is substantial debate over the exact boundaries of the postcolonial field and even the definition of the term 'postcolonial', generally, it refers to the examination of the interactions and relations between European nations and the societies they colonized. The formation of the colony through various systems of control as well as the various stages of the development of anti-colonial feelings interest many academics of the field. Generally, the 'postcolonial' is used to signify a position against imperialism and Eurocentrism (Ashcroft, Griffiths, & Tiffin 1998). Postcolonial literature has given emergence to vigorous discussions. Even as some condemn its elusiveness and lack of historical and material distinctiveness, others reason that most former colonies are far from free of colonial manipulation or domination and thus cannot be postcolonial in the true sense (Tyson 1999). The emphasis on colonizer and colonized relations, moreover, complicates the operation of internal domination within the colonies. Nonetheless, others rebuke the predisposition in the Western academy to be more agreeable to postcolonial literature and theory that is attuned with postmodern formulations while ignoring the critical pragmatism of writers more concerned in the essentials of social and racial oppression (Ashcroft, Griffiths, & Tiffin 1998).

Despite these reservations and debates, research in Postcolonial Studies is growing because postcolonial studies allow for wide-ranging exploration in various contexts. The formation of empire, the impact of colonization on postcolonial history, economy, science, and culture, the cultural productions of colonized societies, feminism and post colonialism, agency for marginalized people, and the state of the post colony in contemporary economic and cultural contexts are some broad topics examined upon in postcolonial studies (Tyson 1999). Postcolonial Theory therefore deals with the reading and writing of literature written in previously or currently colonized countries, or literature written in colonizing countries which deals with colonization or colonized peoples. It focuses particularly on the ways in which literature by the colonizing culture distorts the experience and realities, and inscribes the inferiority, of the colonized people (Barry 1995). In addition to this, the theory focuses upon literature by colonized peoples which attempts to articulate their identity and reclaim their past. It also deals with the way in which literature in colonizing countries appropriate the language, images, scenes and tradition and cultures of colonized countries (Tyson 1999).

At this juncture, it would be important to discuss the relevance of culture in postcolonial contexts. In explaining the relevance of culture, the concept of hybridity is quintessential. Hybridity, is an imperative model in post-colonial theory. Ashcroft, Griffiths, and Tiffin (1998) use this term to refer to the integration or mingling of cultural signs and practices from the colonizing and the colonized cultures. The assimilation and adaptation of cultural practices can be seen as positive, enriching, and dynamic, and at the same time oppressive. Even so, hybridity is useful for helping to break down the false sense that colonized and colonizing cultures are monolithic, or have essential, unchanging features (Ashcroft, Griffiths, & Tiffin 1998). The phenomenon of hybridity more often than not perplexes issues of alienation, marginalization and even otherness. These issues are often characteristic of individuals experiencing transcultural encounters. The protagonist in the novel LDNBTM also faces a similar predicament of being 'othered' emotionally, psychologically and sexually in his attempts to come to terms with his identity and sense of self during his stay in London.

UNDERSTANDING NOTIONS OF IDENTITY THROUGH PSYCHOANALYSIS

The analytical psychology theory was founded by Carl Gustav Jung. For the purpose of this research, the archetypal approach, which is a branch of the analytical psychology theory will be discussed. The aspects of psychology which convey archetypes which will be employed include the personal unconscious, the persona, the shadow and the self. However, the study of aspects of psychology which convey archetypes will not be wholesome without the examination of the collective unconscious. The collective unconscious is vital as it is through the collective unconscious that these aspects of psychology which convey archetypes are brought forth. These aspects of psychology which convey archetypes, in addition to the social identity theory and postcolonial theory, will be helpful in deciphering the feelings and emotions of the protagonist during his adaptation of identity and sense of self under transcultural circumstances in London.

The study of psychology is in point of fact a science, a methodically composed framework of knowledge (Menninger 1974). The rationale of psychology is to assist human beings in controlling themselves more successfully through the awareness of the nature of the human mind. Psychological theories are thus useful in making it possible for us to carry out psychological studies to comprehend the state of mind and behaviour of individuals. The reason behind this is so that we will be competent enough to achieve a better understanding towards the mode in which an individual thinks, behaves, feels and acts. The human personality is strongly linked with psychological states of the mind. Personality can be defined as the characteristics and intrinsic worth of a person, seen as a whole. Personality makes up the qualities that make the individual different from the others. Personality, as the expression of the wholeness of man, is defined by Jung as an adult ideal whose cognisant realisation through individuation is the aspiration of human development in the second half of life (Menninger 1974).

In psychology, there are nine focal approaches towards the study of the personality. They are the psychoanalytic approach, the neopsychoanalytic approach, also known as analytical psychology, the life span approach, the trait approach, the humanistic approach, the cognitive approach, the behavioural approach, the social-learning approach and finally the limited domain approach (Schultz 2001). Sigmund Freud (1856-1939) was the initiator of the first approach of examining the personality through psychoanalysis.

The main outline of the approach is the three structures of the personality, which are the id, ego and superego. The psychoanalysis theory is also extensively used in the study of literature. One of the reasons is to help us grasp the behaviour of humans. This is pertinent, as literature is predominantly about the characters and performance of humans. Nevertheless, it should be pointed out here that literary characters are not subjective and thus do not have psyches that can be evaluated. Instead, literary characters have literary psyches which can be studied. Another rationale behind the use of the psychoanalytical approach is to help elucidate the motivations of authors and present additional knowledge of the way in which literature is used to reach out to readers and the manner in which readers act in response.

JUNGIAN CRITICISM

Jungian criticism of literature departs slightly from psychoanalytic criticism. Jung's criticism, which was influenced by Jungian ideas, principally states that the role of the collective unconscious is seen in the determination of cultural behaviour. Thus, the emphasis of Jung's ideas is not on the individual unconscious, but rather on the collective unconscious. Individuals from all cultures share this collective unconscious. Jung perceives the collective unconscious as 'the repository of racial memories and primordial images and patterns of experience known as archetypes' (Abrams 1999). Unlike Freud who visions literature as a disguised form of libidinal wish fulfilment that parallels the fantasies of a neurotic personality, Jung regards literature as elements whose patterns occur time and again in diverse cultures, which is an exposition of the archetypes of the collective unconscious (Brown 1961). Jung believes that an excellent author possesses and imparts readers' access to the archetypal images, which are deep in the racial memory. Jung's theory has been an immense influence on archetypal criticism and myth criticism.

In Jung's observation, the total personality, also known as the psyche, is made up of a number of distinctive structures that influence one another. These structures include the ego, the personal unconscious and the collective unconscious. The ego is the centre of consciousness, the part of the psyche concerned with perceiving, feeling, and remembering. 'The ego acts in a selective way, admitting into conscious awareness only a portion of the stimuli to which we are exposed' (Schultz 2001:100). The personal unconscious in Jung's system is similar to Freud's conception of the preconscious. According to Jung, 'It is a reservoir of material that was once conscious but has been forgotten or suppressed because it was insignificant or disturbing' (Schultz 2001: 100). The collective unconscious on the other hand is the deepest and least reachable level of the psyche. The collective unconscious is the most controversial aspect of Jung's organization of personality. Ancient experiences contained in the collective unconscious are manifested by recurring themes or patterns acknowledged as archetypes and are passed along from one generation to the other.

Jung asserts that there are four fundamental psychological functions, namely thinking, feeling, sensing and intuiting. Jung classifies people on the base of two attitudes, the extraverted personality and the introverted personality. 'Extraversion is an attitude of the psyche characterised by an orientation towards the external world and other people'. Introversion on the other hand is 'an attitude of the psyche characterised by an orientation towards one's own thoughts and feelings' (Schultz 2001). In other words, extraverts are open, sociable and orientated towards people while introverts are inhibited, timid and have a propensity to focus on themselves, their thoughts and their feelings. The understanding of the extravert and introvert personality is essential as it will help in the analysis of the characters and personality of the unnamed protagonist in *London Does Not Belong to Me*, the main focus of the study. At this juncture, it would be important to note that an important aspect of Jung's approach is the element of archetypes. These elements are the most influential elements in the interpretation of characters in literature as they are closely connected to a literary approach. This approach is known as the archetypal approach.

ARCHETYPAL APPROACH

An archetype is a pattern from which reproductions are made usually similar to the original but not necessarily identical to it. An archetype is thus a prototype or mould capable of change depending on the circumstances. 'It is general and universal, primordial and recurrent'(Rupprecht 1999). Archetypes could come into view as a situation, for instance the quest, various rites of passage, the journey, the fall, death and rebirth, and much more. It can also appear as a symbol or association, for instance light-darkness, water-desert, heaven-hell, and much more. The focus of the study is on the aspects of psychology which convey archetypes present in the novel *London Does Not Belong to Me* with regards to the character of the protagonist and other selected characters. Why do archetypes exist? Carl Jung has made available one possible response to the question of why archetypes subsist. Jung agreed with Freud that man's mind consists of a conscious level and an unconscious level. 'Man's mind is thus like an island in a sea. The land above the water is normal consciousness, the everyday knowing level. However, just beneath the surface lies the personal unconscious, a stage unique in each individual and created by repressed emotions, subliminal receptions, and forgotten occurrences' (Schultz 2001). Below that level is what Jung describes as the "collective unconscious," a level that is shared by all humanity. Freud had only worked with the personal unconscious and its role in psychoanalysis. Thus, in developing the concept of a collective unconscious, Jung went beyond Freud and offered his own distinctive contribution to psychology. Jung tried to provide evidence on the existence of the collective unconscious using dream analysis, as the unconscious manifests itself symbolically in dreams. Despite abundant research, the collective unconscious still remains elusive. It is impossible to define archetypes accurately, as the boundaries or even the true nature of archetypes are not known. Jung argues that 'The primordial image or archetype is a figure, whether it be a demon, man, or process, that repeats itself in the course of history whenever creative fantasy is freely manifested. Essentially, therefore, it is a mythological figure. If we subject these images to a closer examination, we discover them to be the formulated resultants of countless typical experiences of our ancestors. They are, as it were, the psychic residues of numberless experiences of the same type'(Fordham 1966). Thus, archetypes are primordial and universal. Knowledge about the collective unconscious is vital to the study as it will help in the analysis of how characters act, speak, think and dream.

THE COLLECTIVE UNCONSCIOUS AND ARCHETYPES

Jung's theory divides the psyche into three parts. The first is the ego, which Jung identifies with the conscious mind. Closely related is the personal unconscious, which includes anything which is not presently conscious, but can be. The personal unconscious is like most people's understanding of the unconscious in that it includes both memories that are easily brought to mind and those that have been suppressed for some reason (Jung 1964).

Jung adds that the part of the psyche that makes his theory stand out from all others is the collective unconscious. Jung calls the collective unconscious as psychic inheritance. It is the reservoir of our experiences as a species, a kind of knowledge we are all born with (Jung 1964). And yet we can never be directly conscious of it. It influences all of our experiences and behaviours, most especially the emotional ones, but we only know about it indirectly, by looking at those influences. There are some experiences that show the effects of the collective unconscious more clearly than others: The experiences of love at first sight, of déjà vu, and the immediate recognition of certain symbols and the meanings of certain myths, could all be understood as the sudden conjunction of our outer reality and the inner reality of the collective unconscious (Schultz 2001). Grander examples are the creative experiences shared by artists and musicians all over the world and in all times, or the spiritual experiences of mystics of all religions, or the parallels in dreams, fantasies, mythologies, fairy tales, and literature (Jung 1964).

The contents of the collective unconscious are called archetypes. Jung also called them dominants, imagos, mythological or primordial images, and a few other names, but archetypes seem to have won out over these. Archetypes are also acknowledged as original models or prototypes. An archetype is an unlearned tendency to experience things in a certain way. The archetype has no form of its own, but it acts as an "organizing principle" on the things we see or do. 'According to Carl Gustav Jung, archetypes dwell in the unconscious mind of individuals and are inherited from ancestors. Archetypes are symbols, characters, situations and images that can be universally understood. Archetypes structure the collective unconscious, which is a set of primal memories common to all humanity regardless of culture, history and race. It exists in the subconscious mind. All cultures identify with archetypes, as they are universal symbols. The collective unconscious is a product of a collective experience of our forefathers or ancestors. According to Jung, primordial archetypal images are present in individuals even before they are born' (Sivapalan, 2007:128-129). Although the materialization of the idea may be dissimilar, the idea itself is still the same. According to Philip Wheelwright, archetypes are those which carry the same or very similar meanings for a large portion, if not all mankind. It is a discoverable fact that certain symbols, such as the sky father and earth mother, light, blood, up-down, the axis of a wheel, and others, recur again and again in cultures so remote from one another in space and time that there is no likelihood of any historical influence and causal connection among them.

Jung proposed several archetypes, among which are the hero, the mother, the child, God, death, power, and the wise old man (Schultz 2001). Among other notable archetypes are archetypes of facts of life or situations such as love, growing up and loss of innocence. Character archetypes are also popular, for example, the hero, villain, outcast, scapegoat, lovers, shrew, witch, femme fatale, and the devil. Lions, tigers and snakes fall under animal archetypes while the rose, paradise and even seasons fall under the category of nature. The archetype of a journey or quest is yet another important archetype. A few of these archetypes are developed more than others and influence the psyche more consistently. These elements are in essence the aspects of psychology which convey archetypes.

The personal unconscious is a reservoir of materials that was once conscious but has been forgotten or concealed because it was either trivial or upsetting. According to Jung (1964), the personal unconscious stores individually accumulative experiences of the individual. Jung adds that the personal unconscious is used to denote experiences, thoughts and memories that slip out of consciousness and become unconscious. Schultz (2001) observes that the personal unconscious also contains contents that are too unimportant to recall. The collective unconscious is the deepest and most inaccessible level of the psyche. According to Schultz (2001), the collective unconscious is the most unusual and controversial aspect of Jung's theory. The collective unconscious refers to experiences, themes and images which are shared by human. Mankind accumulate these experiences and pass them on to each new generation (Jung 1964). The collective unconscious appears in speech, action and thoughts.

According to Schultz (2001), the persona is a mask or a public face we wear to present ourselves. Jung believed that the persona is indispensable as we are compelled to play many roles in life in order to succeed as well as get along with other people. The persona can both be helpful and harmful at the same time. This is due to the fact that instead of playing a certain role, we may become that particular role. Due to this, certain aspects of our personality may not develop. Although it begins as an archetype, by the time we are finished realizing it, it is the part of us most distant from the collective unconscious. At its best, it is just the good impression we all wish to present as we fill the roles society requires of us. But, of course, it can also be the false impression we use to manipulate people's opinions and behaviours. And, at its worst, it can be mistaken, even by us, for our true nature.

The self is representative of the unity, the wholeness and the integration of the total personality. The goal of life is to realize the self. The self represents the transcendence of all opposites, so that every aspect of the personality is expressed equally. The self is also a point of balance between the polarities of the conscious and the unconscious that form the centre of the psyche (Jung 1964). The self usually imparts a positive influence on the individual.

The most powerful aspect of psychology which conveys archetypes as proposed by Jung is the shadow archetype. This archetype contains the basic, primitive animal instincts and therefore has the deepest roots of all the aspects of psychology which convey archetypes. Evil and immoral behaviours reside in the shadow archetype. In addition to being the source of evil, the shadow is also the source of vitality, spontaneity, creativity and emotion. If the shadow is totally suppressed, the psyche will become dull and lifeless and the personality will become flat. When this happens, the person becomes overpowered by the unconscious (Schultz 2001). Thus, the most basic potential for patterning is the shadow archetype. This is the potential of experiencing the unconscious side of our unique personalities. As we move deeper into the dark side of our personality, identity begins to dissolve into latent dispositions common to all men. We experience the chaos which indicates that we are drawing close to the material structure of psychic life (Jung 1964). This other side may be manifested in a wealth of images. The shadow is also the easiest of the aspects of psychology which convey archetypes for most persons to experience. We tend to see it in others. We also project our dark side onto others and thus interpret them as enemies or as exotic presences that fascinate. We see the shadow everywhere in popular culture. The shadow is the personification of that part of human, psychic possibility that we deny in ourselves and project onto others. The goal of personality integration is to integrate the rejected, inferior side of our life into our total experience and to take responsibility for it (Schultz 2001).

METHODOLOGY OF RESEARCH

This study attempts a multi-dimensional approach to the study of identity and sense of self in Malaysian Literatures in English, incorporating ideas from the postcolonial theory, analytical psychology theory and social theories of identity. This study will focus on the novel *London Does Not Belong to Me*. Details of the novel are as follows:

Name of Text:	London Does Not Belong to Me
Author:	Lee Kok Liang
Year of Publication:	2003
Publisher:	Maya Press Sdn. Bhd.
Number of pages:	287

RATIONALE FOR TEXT SELECTION

The text for this study was selected based upon the following criteria:

- familiarity with the literary traditions of Malaysian literatures in English
- an understanding of the general socio-political as well as historical background of the country of the period in which the text was set in
- interest in the comprehension of the psyche of postcolonial subjects
- interest in the literary creations of Lee Kok Liang
- to create a sense of awareness of the significance of Malaysian literature in English

THEORETICAL FRAMEWORK

The research will be conducted in the form of a textual analysis of the novel *London Does Not Belong to Me*. The focus of the research will be on the notions of identity and sense of self evolving from transcultural experiences. The analysis of the notions of identity and sense of self will be based upon a literary framework formulated here. The following diagram provides a graphic description of the analytical framework.

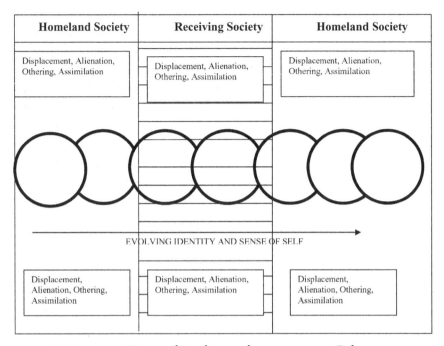

Homeland Society	Receiving Society	Homeland Society

Entry   Transcultural experience   Exit
Homeland cultural experience   Homeland cultural experience

FIGURE 1: Analytical framework

The diagram above 'represents the migratory individual's journey of self-discovery through trans-cultural experiences. The individual's journey of self-discovery is divided into three phases. The first phase represents the individual's point of entry in connection to the cultural experiences of his homeland. The second phase indicates the transcultural experience the individual is confronted with. In the diagram, the individual's transcultural experience is represented by the horizontal lines in the second column. The third phase is the exit phase. This phase is indicative of the protagonist's exit from his transcultural experience and back into the cultural experience of his homeland culture. The circle represents the individual's evolving identity and sense of self from a psychological perspective. These psychological perspectives are made up of the archetypal approach of the analytical psychology theory. These aspects of psychology which convey archetypes include the personal unconscious, the collective unconscious, the persona, the shadow and the self. The empty space in the columns not taken up by the circles represents postcolonial perspectives of the protagonist's negotiation of identity and sense of self. These perspectives include displacement, alienation, othering and assimilation. The arrow beneath the circles indicates that the individual's process of identity negotiation is an evolving one. The aspects of the analytical psychology theory have been chosen as it will be helpful in making sense of the feelings and emotions of the protagonist as he negotiates his identity and sense of self in London. It will also be useful in assisting us with our appreciation of the reason the protagonist spoke, thought and behaved in the ways he did during his process of repositioning of identity and sense of self. Jung's theory was chosen over Freud's theory as the analytical psychology theory is closely related to the literary approach known as archetypal criticism. Jung's emphasis on the collective unconscious as opposed to Freud was also considered in the selection of the analytical psychology approach over other psychoanalytical approaches. With regards to the relations between the self and the society (receiving society and homeland society), aspects of the postcolonial theory that are included are alienation/marginalization, othering, displacement, and assimilation' (Sivapalan, 2007: 130).

The psychological aspects and postcolonial aspects mentioned above will be analysed via personal dimensions, social dimensions and issues that transcend both personal and social dimensions. The personal and social dimensions are projected through elements of culture, race, gender and sexual orientation. Please refer to the Table 1 for a better understanding of the personal and social dimensions that will be used in the analysis.

TABLE 1: Personal and social dimensions used in the analysis of identity and sense of self

Personal dimension	Social dimension	Issues that transcend both dimensions
Gender Sexual orientation	Culture	Race Religion

It must be pointed out here that the individual's interaction between self and psychology represents his repositioning of identity in transcultural experiences on a personal level. His dealings between self and society in the postcolonial context represents the social dimensions of his adaptation of identity. The analysis of the protagonist's identity and sense of self will be based on the elements projected in Table 2.

Table 2: Perspectives analysed

Analytical psychology perspective (Archetypal Perspective)	Postcolonial Perspective

1. **Personal Unconscious**
   Culture and the personal unconscious
   Race and the personal unconscious
   Gender and the personal unconscious
   Sexual orientation and the personal unconscious
2. **Collective Unconscious**
   Culture and the collective unconscious
   Race and the collective unconscious
   Gender and the collective unconscious
   Sexual orientation and the collective unconscious
3. **Persona**
   Culture and the persona
   Race and the persona
   Gender and the persona
   Sexual orientation and the persona
4. **Shadow**
   Culture and the shadow
   Race and the shadow
   Gender and the shadow
   Sexual orientation and the shadow
5. **Self**
   Culture and the self
   Race and the self
   Gender and the self
   Sexual orientation and the self
	1. **Displacement**
	   Culture and displacement
	   Race and displacement
	   Gender and displacement
	   Sexual orientation and displacement
	2. **Alienation/marginalization**
	   Culture and alienation/marginalization
	   Race and alienation/marginalization
	   Gender and alienation/marginalization
	   Sexual orientation and alienation/marginalization
	3. **Othering**
	   Culture and othering
	   Race and othering
	   Gender and othering
	   Sexual orientation and othering
	4. **Assimilation**
	   Culture and assimilation
	   Race and assimilation
	   Gender and assimilation
	   Sexual orientation and assimilation

MODE OF ANALYSIS

This section will discuss the manner in which the analysis of the protagonist's negotiation of identity and sense of self will take place. Table 2 provides a graphic description of the mode of analysis.

TABLE 3: Mode of analysis

Analytical Domain	Archetypal Approach	Postcolonial Approach	Social Identity Constructs	Summary
Personal a) Gender b) Sexual orientation	Personal unconscious Collective Unconscious Persona Shadow Self	Displacement Alienation/ Marginalization Othering Assimilation	Acceptance Rejection Transnationalism Categorization Identification Comparison	Summary of findings
Social a) Culture	Personal unconscious Collective Unconscious Persona Shadow Self	Displacement Alienation/ Marginalization Othering Assimilation	Acceptance Rejection Transnationalism Categorization Identification Comparison	Summary of findings
Issues that transcend both personal and social domains a) Race	Personal unconscious Collective Unconscious Persona Shadow Self	Displacement Alienation/ Marginalization Othering Assimilation	Acceptance Rejection Transnationalism Categorization Identification Comparison	Summary of findings

The study of the human identity has long intrigued scholars and academicians of various fields, be it a scientific or literary area. This interest in identity has sparked of numerous theoretical developments in the hopes of comprehending the true essence of the human kind and of his thoughts, his feelings and his emotion wellbeing. Studies on identity have been done on individual basis and even on collective basis. More often than not, the outcome of these studies has proven breakthrough results and has provided yet another milestone in the understanding of the human identity.

NEGOTIATING CHALLENGES OF IDENTITY AND SENSE OF SELF UNDER TRANSCULTURAL CIRCUMSTANCES

INTRODUCTION

This analysis aims at identifying the manner in which the protagonist negotiates challenges to his identity and sense of self under transcultural circumstances. The analysis will be carried out using the archetypal approach from the analytical psychology theory as well as the postcolonial approach. Elements of the archetypal approach, which will be used in the analysis, include the personal unconscious, the collective unconscious, the persona, the shadow and the self. Aspects of the postcolonial theory, which will be used in the analysis, are displacement, alienation/marginalization, othering and assimilation. The archetypes and postcolonial elements listed above will be used to analyse the protagonist's evolving identity and sense of self from the aspects of culture, race, gender and sexual orientation.

SYNOPSIS OF NOVEL

LDNBTM is a novel that highlights the life of migratory or expatriate individuals in London. The characters and events that take place in the novel are very similar to the people and situations that Lee Kok Liang may have encountered during his years in London. These similarities suggest that the novel could be semi-autobiographical in nature. The characters in the novel include the protagonist, Beatrice, Cordelia, Arlette, Guy, Tristam and Steve. The protagonist is a Straits Chinese Malaysian male who goes to London to pursue his studies. Strangely enough, the protagonist is left nameless throughout the novel. Beatrice is an Australian woman whom the protagonist knows from his studies in Sydney. Cordelia and Arlette are Beatrice's housemates. Tristam is an English homosexual and the president of the League of Coloured People. Guy is a Frenchman. He is introduced to the protagonist by Tristam. Steve is an Australian bisexual. He is Tristam's partner for a short duration.

This novel is about the protagonist who leaves his homeland Malaya for a few years to pursue his education in London. In London, he meets Beatrice, his former classmate while studying in Australia. Through Beatrice, he is introduced to Cordelia, Tristam, Ken and

Steve. The protagonist instantly feels attracted to Cordelia. This attraction later leads to a relationship. However, the relationship does not last long as Cordelia suddenly leaves the protagonist and her housemates Beatrice and Arlette. Cordelia does not reveal the reason for her sudden disappearance and does not even leave them with the smallest clue regarding her whereabouts. The novel ends with the protagonist's return to Malaya. As Tristam sends him off, he presents the protagonist with a book titled *London Belongs to Me.* The novel also ends leaving readers to contemplate what the protagonist would do upon his return to his homeland.

THE ANALYSIS

This section contains the analysis of the novel. The analysis has been divided into two main sections. The first section will deal with psychological perspectives while the second section will explore postcolonial perspectives.

ARCHETYPAL PERSPECTIVES TO IDENTITY AND SENSE OF SELF IN TRANSCULTURAL EXPERIENCES

This section will contain an analysis of the protagonist's sense of identity and self from a psychological perspective. The psychoanalytical features of personal unconscious, collective unconscious, persona, shadow and self will be used to explore the protagonist's identity and sense of self in the context of culture, race, gender and sexual orientation by analysing his speech, thoughts and actions.

PERSONAL UNCONSCIOUS AND TRANSCULTURAL EXPERIENCES

The personal unconscious is often linked to materials that were once conscious to an individual but has been forgotten or suppressed. The personal unconscious is thus related to the memory of the individual.

The personal unconscious state may be detected in the following situations:

a) loss of past memory, i.e. memories which are easily forgotten
b) incidents that can be recalled

There are some indications of the personal unconscious in the protagonist of LDNBTM. However, the manifestations of the personal unconscious could only be found in aspects of culture and sexual orientation. Examples of the protagonist's manifestations of personal unconscious with regards to the element of culture are discussed in the sections below.

CULTURE AND THE PERSONAL UNCONSCIOUS

The personal unconscious in the protagonist does not manifest through lost memories of his past but through recollections of memories of his homeland, Malaya. The protagonist's personal unconscious is also evident when thoughts of Cordelia come to his mind. Several instances could be found in relation to culture in the protagonist's personal unconscious.

The protagonist recalls that in his homeland, the people were soft-spoken and very accommodative to the views and opinions of the others. In London however, the communicative culture of the people was different. People were very judgemental of the opinions of their friends. The protagonist reacts to such a situation when he says *I was used to polite talk from others* (pg 99). The protagonist's reference to 'others' is in relation to characters like Beatrice, Cordelia and Tristam. The protagonist readily recalls the communicative culture of his homeland because he feels that people at home were polite and tolerant to the others. Face value is an important element in the communicative culture of the homeland culture of the protagonist. Face value is representative of the notion of dignity, especially among the Chinese community in the protagonist's homeland culture. As a Malaysian Chinese, it is rather natural that this culture is embedded deeply in him. Thus, he finds it difficult to comprehend the coarse speaking mannerism of the West. This is evident when the protagonist says, *there were times when I resented this* (pg 99). He seems to acknowledge the speaking mannerisms of the western society as a threat to his face value and his individuality. This cultural difference between the West and the East creates a conflict in him. The conflict faced by the protagonist suggests that his historical identity is still linked to his native land.

Lee Kok Liang's infusion of the influence of local Malaysian colour is seen at this juncture. The inclusion of the social customs of the immigrant Chinese Malaysian is apparent when the protagonist realises the importance of face value. Thus, it can be deduced that Lee Kok Liang's infusion of such customs are reflective of his writing influences, which he inserts very subtly into LDNBTM.

However, it is felt that although Beatrice, Cordelia and Tristam are not of the same culture as the protagonist, they treat him with respect because they value his friendship and do not want to hurt his feelings. For instance, whenever the protagonist visits Beatrice unannounced, she always welcomed him to her house with a sense of warmth that made the protagonist feel at ease with her. This is exemplified in this statement: *Beatrice spoke rapidly, walking towards me, brushing me with words, dusting away specks of nervousness that clung to me* (pg 12).

Cordelia also influences the protagonist and his personal unconscious. The protagonist's attraction to Cordelia encourages him to introduce her to the culture and traditions of his homeland by acts such as cooking her a Malaysian meal. Here his personal unconscious makes him recall the scenes of the bazaar that are famous features in Malaya and he visualises her in the scene. This is evident in the following extract, *I saw her, a pale figure with milky transparent skin, moving about the hawkers in the bazaar, selecting five-cents worth of chillies and spices from a woman sitting behind rows of cut-away banana leaves in one of the stalls* (pg 84).

The recollection of this particular memory could have been sparked by the protagonist's sense of longing for his homeland. This thought could also suggest his aspirations of taking her to Malaya with the idea of settling down with her there. It is felt that his attraction for Cordelia could be because she was the only white woman to show any interest in him. However, the protagonist's desires to introduce Cordelia to the culture of his homeland prove futile when he notices that even a discussion of the conditions at home make her uncomfortable. *But I have never told her about such things because once I mentioned the sanitary conditions out home, and her face grew solemn, and for the rest of the evening she became morose* (pg 84).

Cordelia's concept of the East as chaotic, irrational, weak, evil and backward are exemplified through her unenthusiastic facial expressions and glum expressions. Cordelia's actions disappoint the protagonist but he does not make his displeasure obvious to her as he secretly hopes that he would still be able to convince her at some point of time. This could be because the protagonist feels that there is an opportunity for him to make Cordelia understand the norms and practices of the culture of his homeland. The protagonist tries to mould Cordelia's personal identity by introducing the culture of Malaya with the hope that she would derive part of her self-concept from his culture. The protagonist's attempts at moulding her self-concept to complement his Asian concept of self could be because he hopes to take her back to Malaya to build a life together with him. The protagonist's wishes remain a dream. This is because Cordelia rejects the protagonist's attempts at forming her individual characteristics. This rejection is reflective of Cordelia's strong sense of self that permeates from her belief that the West is more superior to the East.

Thus, it can be concluded that cultural differences between the protagonist's Eastern beliefs and the Western ideology he is confronted with as a result of transculturalism, creates a conflict of identity within him. This conflict in identity places him at a point of confusion.

SEXUAL ORIENTATION AND THE PERSONAL UNCONSCIOUS

The protagonist's manifestation of the personal unconscious is evident in his sexual orientation. He retracts memories of his homeland during his secret courtship with Cordelia. This is evident in the incident where Cordelia invites him for a walk, under the pretence of showing him around the place she lived. However, the walk turns into an intimate moment when Cordelia allows the protagonist to kiss her. The intimate moment they share creates a sense of joy leading to a recollection of the protagonist's joyful moments when he was in Malaya. The protagonist associates the sense of joy he experiences with Cordelia to his leisurely hours alone, by the beach in his homeland. Both situations evoke in him feelings of tranquillity and peace.

It should be noted here that the examination of the personal unconscious could only be discussed from two aspects: culture and sexual orientation. Furthermore, the protagonist's personal unconscious is only apparent in his thoughts but not in his action and speech. This could be due to the fact that the personal unconscious is a process in which the individual recollects incidents of his past. Thus, the production of action and speech by the protagonist are not crucial features of manifestations. It is also necessary to highlight the fact that the protagonist's personal unconscious only appears in his narrated thought. The manifestations of the protagonist's personal unconscious through his thoughts seem to suggest that the protagonist still feels attachment to Malaya. However, he could also be suppressing his thoughts because he fears that if he makes his thoughts vocal, it could have a negative impact on his relationship with Cordelia. His fear is reasonable because he had already received an unfavourable reaction from her when he brought up the discussion of his country. Not wanting to lose the only white woman who shows interest in him, he suppresses his thoughts of his homeland. Also, the protagonist's suppressed thoughts of Malaya could also be a result of him not wanting to estrange himself from his host. The protagonist's unwillingness to estrange himself from the host culture is symbolic of his trials at assimilating with the host society. His actions connote the element of social identity theory that advocates the notion that when an individual belongs to a group, he is likely to derive his sense of identity or part of his identity from that group. As the protagonist assumes that he belongs to the in-group of the subculture of the receiving society, he tries to maintain his stand with the host society by suppressing his thoughts of his homeland. This suppression is reflective of him trying to upkeep the sense of identity he has derived thus far as a result of his associations with members of the host society.

However, his actions convey negative connotations as it indicates he is ashamed of the conditions of his homeland. Thus, it is felt that he suppresses his thoughts in order to conceal his embarrassment. The fact that he recollects thoughts of his home may be taken to suggest that his sense of identity and self is still linked to his homeland. The analysis suggests that the protagonist does not internalize the norms of the host culture wholly, but uses the host culture norms as a yardstick to the formulation of his evolving identity and sense of self.

COLLECTIVE UNCONSCIOUS AND TRANSCULTURAL EXPERIENCES

The collective unconscious of the protagonist will be analysed through his speech, thoughts and actions. His collective unconscious will be examined from cultural, racial and sexual perspectives.

CULTURE AND THE COLLECTIVE UNCONSCIOUS

The protagonist's collective unconscious is seen at play in several situations in the novel. For instance, the attention and interest paid to him by white women make him very uncomfortable and makes him self-conscious. This is evident when the protagonist says, *Besides, too, most girls made me conscious of myself* (pg 16). The protagonist feels self-conscious under these circumstances because his collective unconscious disapproves of the female being the hegemonic power in a relationship between a man and a woman. The idea that the woman was the 'other' to the male seems to be ingrained in his collective unconscious. Thus, when the protagonist is faced with a situation where the woman makes the first move, his collective unconscious immediately manifests indications of disapproval of such behaviour and even frightens him. The protagonist seems conscious that he comes from a culture, which holds the male in a higher position to the female. Thus, when he is confronted with the situation where he is asked out by women, the protagonist's familiarity with patriarchal practices in his homeland makes it a problem for him to adjust to the western concept of gender equality.

The protagonist's collective unconscious is also embedded with the notion that promiscuous sex and sex before marriage is a forbidden act. The protagonist is conscious that if the men in his society have the urge to commit adultery or forgo their virginity, they should try all means of suppressing their urges. The protagonist's consciousness is evident when he says, *When I left home I was not old enough to have a girl, which in the parts I came from meant marrying. Of course, I did have the urges, but I had disciplined my passion until it became a fine art . . .'* (pg 16).

It is felt that the protagonist's Buddhist norms and systems of belief restricted him from having sexual relations before marriage, as it was unacceptable. Thus, the protagonist's fear of accumulating sin restrains him from committing such acts in his homeland. The protagonist's fear and acts of restraining himself from falling into the trap of the host culture is reflective of his phase of rejection of the culture of the host society. At this point, the protagonist seems to experience the stage of separatism in his development of identity. The stage of separatism influences him to reject certain norms of the host society, for instance the western concept of gender equality.

The protagonist however does not adhere to this practice of his homeland. It is felt that the protagonist's change of beliefs is caused by the release of his id. The protagonist compromises his religious beliefs when he goes to London to accommodate with the host culture. As the protagonist is in a culture that views promiscuous behaviour as acceptable, he engages in the pleasures of the flesh, which is forbidden in the culture of his homeland. The intimate sexual relationships the protagonist has with Cordelia and Beatrice is proof of his disregard of acceptable homeland culture.

The extending of polite behaviour to an older person or any individual regardless of race and religious beliefs is another element that is embedded within the collective unconscious of the protagonist. When he is challenged with a situation in which an older woman glared at him *with a terrible contemptuous sweep in her eyes* (pg 142) when he goes into a shop to buy some food, manifestations of the notion of politeness from his collective unconscious stops him from confronting the woman, even though it is a 'nasty moment'. His politeness could have been the result of ancestral cultural influences, which still remain intact within him. It is felt that his submissive attitude during the situation could also be motivated by another factor. The protagonist remained quite throughout the situation because he did not want to create trouble for himself in a country and culture alien to him. The protagonist's actions could therefore be deemed as self-preservation. His actions could also be provoked by the element of saving his face from being shamed by the white woman. The element of saving face is another influence of his Chinese culture. The element of 'save face', which is embedded in his psyche, reflects that cultural influences of his homeland are more fervent than the cultural influences of the receiving society.

RACE AND THE COLLECTIVE UNCONSCIOUS

The protagonist's judgements about characters of different religion and race are also passed onto him by his ancestors. One such character he judges is Derek. According to the protagonist, *Derek had a clinging pertinacity, so unlike the British in his social relationships* (pg 183). The protagonist experiences Derek's clingy personality when the two of them travel to Paris together. Derek keeps following the protagonist wherever he goes and even stays in the same hotel room with him, much to the displeasure of the protagonist. The protagonist's perception of the British individual could not have been a product of his own deductions during his stay in London as he was still in the initial stages of learning and discovering about the host society. Thus it would be impossible for him to make such fervent statements of Derek with insufficient knowledge on the manner in which the British related socially with other individuals. It is felt that the protagonist's knowledge of the British individual's social relationship patterns could have been passed on to him from his ancestors who were once colonised by the British.

SEXUAL ORIENTATION AND THE COLLECTIVE UNCONSCIOUS

Although the conception that any form of sexual relationship between a man and woman is prohibited until they are legally married is embedded in the protagonist's collective unconscious, he seems to reject this philosophy. This is apparent in the scene where the protagonist insists on combing Cordelia's hair for her. It is felt that the protagonist's insistence in helping Cordelia with the combing of her hair is a result of his inquisitiveness, and an experimentation of sexuality. The protagonist is aware that if he were back in his homeland, he would never be able to perform such acts on a woman he has no family ties with. Thus, the protagonist uses this opportunity to gain sexual experiences, which he could never perform openly in his homeland. It is felt that the protagonist is, at this point, playing with the notion of the exotic as advocated by Said's Orientalism. The protagonist's actions however reflect reverse orientalism because his behaviour is indicative of the postcolonial individual taking control over the colonial. The protagonist views Cordelia as an exotic being.

Manifestations of the collective unconscious are viewed in cultural, racial and sexual aspects. The research shows that there are instances in which the protagonist adheres to the norms of his collective unconscious. However, there are also situations where the protagonist ignores these manifestations. These rejections are ascribed to his sense of curiosity of the cultural, racial and sexual habits of the host culture. Hence, when the protagonist closes his eyes to the voice of his collective unconscious, he could be undertaking the process of cultural accommodation. This process of selection is the practice transculturalism advocates.

Nevertheless, the protagonist's rejection of certain manifestations of his collective unconscious could also be attributed to the fact that he is an immigrant Malaysian Chinese. Being an immigrant Malaysian Chinese, the ancestral influence on him is not as strong as the impact it produced. His exposure to education could also be a contributing factor towards rejection of certain manifestations of his collective unconscious.

It can be concluded that for the protagonist, his culture is confined geographically. Being in London makes it easy for the protagonist to divert from the things he was restricted to in Malaya, for instance the combing of a woman's hair. This suggests that the protagonist's weak identity and sense of self is the result of the lack of affliction to homeland culture. There is also a strong suggestion of a clash between his id and his superego. In some situations, the protagonist's id seems to prevail as animalistic and sexual instinct. The protagonist's id seems to prevail because the superego manifested in the host society condones greater freedom for individuality and personal pleasures, thus satisfying the id.

PERSONA AND TRANSCULTURAL EXPERIENCES

The persona is an important manifestation of the collective unconscious. The persona is a social mask worn by individuals to portray the various social roles they play in their daily lives. This social mask worn by individuals help them succeed in life and even get along with people. In LDNBTM, the persona of the protagonist is seen at play in the aspects of culture and sexual orientation.

CULTURE AND THE PERSONA

The protagonist's persona is manifested from his collective unconscious when he hides his true emotions when he converses with his friends. The hiding of his feelings is seen when he suppresses his shame for not being able to talk the language of the host country fluently. He conceals his feelings to play the role of a polite houseguest in Beatrice's house. The protagonist feels that he has to hide his feelings of embarrassment because he is incompetent in the English language. As the English language poses as a barrier to communication, he often feels disgraced and small when he is not able to speak as fluently as his friends. To camouflage his weakness, the protagonist *suppressed the desire to talk on serious subjects and avoided saying anything really offensive* (pg 25).

The protagonist also 'became an agreeable man' (pg 26), refusing to contradict anyone directly on the grounds of insulting them and their culture, thus resorting to express his ideas in a 'roundabout manner'. He does not seem to pay too much attention to his conversational capabilities and accepts it as 'an easy way out' (pg 26) to deal with situations that require him to voice his thoughts and opinions. Such actions reflect his attempts at conformity with the host culture. Conformity is seen when he pretends to be an agreeable man to prove to his friends that he could associate himself with their norms. However, it is suspected that the protagonist behaves in such a manner to avoid being alienated and othered by his friends. It could also be because he wanted them to acknowledge and accept him into their in-group.

During the party held in Tristam's house, the protagonist plays the role of a good party guest although he feels 'completely isolated' (pg 55). He satisfies his host and the other guests by having a drink of beer and mingling with the different groups of people who come to the party. When he sees Steve's arm around Cordelia's waist, the protagonist becomes agitated as he is of the assumption that Cordelia belongs to him. Furthermore, his collective unconscious makes him aware that it is inappropriate for a woman (in the culture of his homeland) to be intimate with another person of the opposite gender if she was already in an existing relationship. Although the protagonist feels disturbed by the development, he presents a calm composure. The social mask worn by the protagonist not only helps him save face but also adapt to the situation.

Pretentiousness and lies are other modes with which the persona functions. The protagonist's persona is evident when he pretends to be interested in Tristam's ramblings. The protagonist is of the opinion that Tristam expresses himself in an abstract manner and this does not appeal much to the protagonist. Not wanting to hurt Tristam's feelings, the protagonist often agrees with Tristam's views and feelings on the various subjects they discuss. An example of this is provided here:

> *Tristam: If you've read Cocteau you will understand. I can't express myself better.*
>
> *Protagonist: I'm sorry, I haven't read it.*
>
> *Tristam: For heaven's sake, don't apologise (he raised his voice) If you haven't read it, all right, all right. But it's a strain on me trying to explain things.*
>
> *So terrible, human communication (he rubbed his temples furiously) I don't know how. Just don't know how.*
>
> *Protagonist: I understand you (I said trying to please him).*

(pg 131)

It is clear from the extract above that the manifestation of the persona in the protagonist helps him lie to Tristam. In addition to guiding Tristam to end the conversation successfully, the protagonist has also strengthened his friendship with Tristam. Thus, it cannot be denied that the persona is an important feature of the human psyche. Nevertheless, it is felt that the protagonist's ability to make Tristam end his conversation is reflective of the postcolonial individual's shrewdness in outwitting and manipulating the coloniser. However, the protagonist does not put his ability to good use. This could be because he is too absorbed with the notion of assimilating with the host society and fears that he would be alienated by his friends. Here, the protagonist's identity and sense of self is at the stage of conformity where the postcolonial individuals judge themselves through the lens of the host culture.

SEXUAL ORIENTATION AND THE PERSONA

The protagonist's sexual orientation also evokes his persona. His relationships with Cordelia and Beatrice manifest the persona from his collective unconscious. In his relationship with Cordelia, the protagonist sometimes pretends to be happy when he is with her. This is evident in his thoughts: *I did not feel like laughing. But I could not help myself* (pg 58). It is obvious that the protagonist forces himself to portray a sense of contentment when he is with Cordelia because he does not want to destroy his relationship with her. Although he thinks that Cordelia's ways were not always amusing, the persona in him motivates him to hide his true feelings so that he may please her. The protagonist's actions could be because he does not want to lose the sexual attention he gets from Cordelia. It appears that the protagonist's nature seems to cloud his ability to rationalize.

The protagonist's persona manifests yet again when he is with Beatrice. Even though the protagonist is 'repelled by the sight' (pg 105) of Beatrice, he continues seeing her. To avoid hurting her feelings, the protagonist puts on the pretence of enjoying her company. He feels indebted to her because it is through Beatrice that he meets and falls in love with Cordelia. It is also through Beatrice that the protagonist learns how to live in a country that is alien to him. It is felt that that the protagonist's appreciation towards Beatrice is borne out of his self-interaction between himself and the receiving society. This self-interaction affects him and instils a sense of gratitude towards Beatrice.

The findings show that the manifestations of the persona from the protagonist's collective unconscious affected him positively as well as negatively. The positive outcome of the manifestations of the persona helps the protagonist get along with the people in London. The mask he wears assists him further in adjusting to life and achieving his goals. The negative effect of the persona is seen when the persona encourages him to hide his emotions, lie and pretend to be what he is not. The research shows that the manifestation of the persona in the protagonist influences him to act in the manner he does at conscious and unconscious levels. His eagerness to be accepted into the host culture and his fear of being deemed an outcast further promote the persona archetype.

THE SHADOW AND TRANSCULTURAL EXPERIENCES

This section will examine the manifestation of the shadow archetype in the protagonist. The shadow embodies evil and immoral features of the psyche. When the shadow goes out of control, self-destruction is imminent. The manifestation of the shadow is also through the collective unconscious and can be examined via the individual's speech, actions and thoughts.

CULTURE AND SHADOW

The manifestation of the shadow archetype in the protagonist can be seen in his conversation with Guy. The protagonist's shadow is seen at play when he manipulates Guy to seek information about Cordelia:

> 'Did Steve have a girl with him'? I asked in a very low voice. Guy however did not hear me. He was thinking too. So I had to ask the question again.
>
> 'A girl with him'? Guy showed some surprise. 'No, he was alone. Why do you ask that'?
>
> 'I just ask'. I put a stupid smile on my face. 'Well they say Paris is full of girls' (pg 139).

It is felt that the protagonist mimics the 'scheming' characteristics of the coloniser when he manipulates Guy into telling him what he knows of Cordelia's whereabouts. It seems that the protagonist has absorbed certain norms of the host culture. His identity seems to be influenced by the stage of acceptance in which he internalizes the ideologies of domination. It is felt that the protagonist's internalization of the domination ideology of the colonizer is influenced by his shadow, which is embedded with negative thoughts. When these negative thoughts spiral out of control, the shadow overpowers his ego. The ego is the element of the human psyche, which controls the individual's feelings and senses. When the shadow overpowers the ego, self-destruction is the forthcoming result. In the situation above, the protagonist's shadow is yet to empower his ego fully. Thus, it can be concluded that the protagonist's self is yet to be tarnished.

RACE AND SHADOW

The protagonist begins to harbour ill feelings for Tristam when the latter uses him and Gopal as show items in a meeting session of the League of Coloured People. Tristam was the leader of the league. Being the leader, Tristam took it upon himself to educate the non-white individuals who were members of his group. When Tristam extends him invitation to a session at the club, the protagonist accepts it to satisfy Tristam. However, the manner in which Tristam conducts himself during the meeting and the way he treats the members of his club angers the protagonist. This is evident when the protagonist narrates the following: *I began resenting Tristam for sitting us together as if we were a pair of guinea pigs* (pg 145). It is felt that the protagonist's annoyance is due to the fact that he feels Tristam marginalizes him. These ill feelings are created by the protagonist's shadow. This marginalized feeling is also a result of his status as the 'other' in the host society. In addition, Tristam who symbolizes the West has the power to make the protagonist see and experience himself as the 'other' as a result of inner compulsion. It is felt that the protagonist's marginalised feeling is a result of this inner compulsion, which compels him to feel marginalized.

Another example of the manifestation of the shadow archetype with regards to race is seen when he goes shopping at Whiteley's. In this situation, the protagonist is treated in a rude manner by a woman customer because he is not British. The following extract exemplifies the situation from page 142:

But once, I remembered I, was not so fortunate. Was it at Whiteley's, when trying to buy a packet of chicken noodle soup in a hurry? I had pushed my hand absent-mindedly over the counter, when I noticed a thin woman, very sharp in the face, glaring at me, and after looking me over with a terrible contemptuous sweep of her eyes, she leant back against her male companion, turning her old face to him, with a put-on smile, whereupon the young man kissed her on the cheeks. Satisfied, she threw me a glance as if to say, 'Get out of my way'. It was a nasty moment for me, and although in my mind I shouted curses, my manner was mild. She walked off triumphantly holding her shopping bag in her hand.

When the woman throws the protagonist an angry expression, it ignites dissatisfaction in him. This sense of displeasure in the manner in which he is treated by the white woman invokes negative thoughts in him. These negative thoughts manifested through his shadow makes him curse the white woman. However, he does not verbally demonstrate his resentment to her. The protagonist represses his resentment because he is afraid of being alienated by the host culture. This fear, which is born out of his inner compulsion, changes his identity, making him less secure of his self. However, the protagonist's act of repressing his resentment could also be a result of him striving to be accepted by the host society. This strain, which he consciously takes onto himself, makes him adapt and change in order to see himself as a presence in the host society. This strain is essential to the protagonist's process of identity repositioning and construction.

GENDER AND SHADOW

The shadow archetype is also evident in the protagonist's dealings with the aspect of gender. Two incidents were identified in the course of the research. In the first, the protagonist mocks Steve and Tristam for being gay though he never expresses his thoughts verbally. The reason for these cynical thoughts about the gay lovers stems from Steve's comment of the protagonist when the latter is drunk. The protagonist becomes angry for being called *a very intriguing person* (pg 69). In defence of his self-esteem he says, *But I am not, I am not (a very intriguing person), I tried to say. I waved my arm and gave a crazy smile. I knew how I looked to them. Small, taut, dark. But I am not* (pg 69).

When the protagonist does not get any reply from Steve, he becomes more irritated. His drunken condition makes matters worse for him as his friends think that he is behaving in an inappropriate manner. Even so, the protagonist does not seem to be bothered that he is making a fool of himself although he was aware of it. The lack of concern for his reputation and neglect of his own face are manifestations of the shadow archetype in him. The protagonist's harsh comment of Tristam is a product of the shadow archetype that embeds malevolent thoughts in him. The protagonist's actions of passing negative comments of gay men are reflective of his resistance of the host culture. This resistance is reflective of the stage of redefinition in the protagonist's process of identity development. This sense of resistance gives him the strength to challenge gay relationships in the dominant host culture.

SEXUAL ORIENTATION AND SHADOW

The manifestation of the shadow in the protagonist is perpetrated by his thoughts of losing Cordelia. Cordelia has the ability to pull the starter of the protagonist's engine that helps him *come to life with a shuddering motion* (pg 58). When Cordelia leaves him, the protagonist is in a dilemma as Cordelia makes him feel more complete. At a certain point, the protagonist becomes disoriented and loses his sense of rationality. This loss of rationality is the beginning of the manifestation of ill thoughts and actions in the protagonist. This is projected in the manifestation of his shadow.

A good example of the manifestation of evil and immoral thoughts in the protagonist is seen in his treatment of Beatrice. For instance, the protagonist vents his frustration on Beatrice upon learning that Cordelia has left him. The act of losing one's rationality is an act driven by the shadow.

The protagonist's immoral behaviour towards Beatrice, which is a manifestation of the shadow archetype, is also portrayed when he starts to avoid her on purpose. This is evident in the following extracts:

- *I stammered out a reply, making excuses and fearful of asking her the one question on my mind. I promised to call on her the next week; but now I was so busy getting my papers and files in order* (pg 79).
- *I had avoided her for the past weeks as I had no intention of continuing with our relationships* (pg 105).

Beatrice's glances at him also stir negative feelings in the protagonist. The protagonist feels 'uncomfortable' (pg 104) when Beatrice gives him intense looks. In the third incident, the manifestation of the shadow in the protagonist is seen when the protagonist narrates the following, *I needed Beatrice as a stimulant to keep my love fresh. Whether she had any intimation that I had been using her as a fire poker to rake up the embers, uncovering the globs of burning coal beneath the ashes of time and forgetfulness, I did not know* (pg 156).

The ill manner in which the protagonist treats Beatrice is a result of his shadow embedding negative thoughts and feelings in him. As a result, the protagonist resorts to confronting Beatrice in a harsh manner. His selfishness makes him neglect Beatrice's feelings and the other friends like Tristam and Guy who were close to him. Thus, it can be concluded that the protagonist's shadow weakens his ego, almost leading him to self-destruction. This dampens his efforts at repositioning his identity and sense of self.

THE SELF AND TRANSCULTURAL EXPERIENCES

The self is representative of all positive associations in the human psyche. The self assists the individual in achieving a goal or dreams. When an Individual takes steps to upgrade himself, it is his self, which helps him along this process. In addition to being the element that encourages compassion and sympathy, the self has the ability to make an individual feel a sense of remorse for performing actions that were considered wrong. The full realization of the self is only achieved in future events that are to take place in the life of the individual.

CULTURE AND THE SELF

The protagonist's negotiation with his self and culture is seen when he accompanies Tristam to visit Gopal (an Indian settled in Africa who is a friend of Tristam and the protagonist) in the Dartford asylum. As they settle themselves in the ward, Tristam pulls out a photograph of Gandhi from his wallet. The protagonist is aware of the fact that the picture of Gandhi could provoke Gopal's anger. To prevent Gopal from getting angry and hurting himself, the protagonist *swiftly reached out and pushed the photograph back'* (pg 175) into Tristam's wallet. The protagonist tells Tristam, *Tris, you just don't understand. It'll be just too terrible* (pg 175). The protagonist's actions are also motivated by his knowledge of Gopal's culture and beliefs. The protagonist seems to be sensitive towards Gopal's culture as both share a similar ideology. It is felt that his compassion for Gopal is influenced by his homeland culture that emphasises respect for traditions and religious beliefs of other races. His formation of identity and sense of self is seen to be at the stage of redefinition as he is no longer compelled to conform to the host culture. His actions also denote that he attempts to overcome thoughts of intimidation by the host society to establish a stronger sense of self.

GENDER AND THE SELF

When Steve tries to seduce the protagonist, the latter does not brush him off in a violent manner. Instead, the protagonist declines Steve's advances in a nonchalant and polite manner. The protagonist's casual outlook of the situation could have been motivated by the fact that he sympathises with the gay community. As Steve is an acquaintance, the protagonist's sympathy for him is heightened. Not wanting to hurt his feelings, the protagonist rejects him in a courteous and respectful manner. The protagonist's courteous, sympathetic and respectful sense of self is a result of the positive qualities embedded in his psyche as well as a growing sense of belief in him. This growing sense of belief in him is symbolic of the stage of integration in the protagonist's development and formation of identity. His actions of coming to terms with gay practices in the host society indicate that the protagonist is able to integrate belonging to the dominant culture.

SEXUAL ORIENTATION AND THE SELF

The protagonist's guilty feelings are manifested through the self. But, the protagonist thinks that it is Cordelia who helps him awaken his sense of guilt. This is evident when he says, *Cordelia had infected me with a sense of guilt that had lain concealed* (pg 30). Thus, it is apparent that Cordelia has a strong control over the emotions of the protagonist. When she leaves him, the protagonist becomes devastated. Sensing that he is distressed by the whole incident, the protagonist realises that it would only be proper for him to take charge of his own feelings. This sense of realization is actually a manifestation of the protagonist's self to rid himself of negative emotions. This realization also makes him a more optimistic person.

Optimism is another quality brought forth by the self. The protagonist's optimism is seen in the following extract: *I found that I could will myself into the belief that one day, perhaps tomorrow, she would write to me . . .* (pg 98). It is felt that the protagonist's optimism is born of his realization of his sense of self. The protagonist's sense of self is showcased most prominently when he comes to realize that the love he had for Cordelia was merely based on lustful desire. He realizes that his chase for Cordelia is pointless. He also finally comprehends that Beatrice's love for him is genuine. His conscience makes him aware that he treated Beatrice wrongfully on many occasions. His sense of guilt also prompts him to accept Beatrice's love.

From the extract, it can be summarised that Beatrice plays an important role in helping the protagonist come to terms with his true sense of self. Although the protagonist feels that Cordelia is his source of inspiration of self-attainment, his calculations prove wrong. However, it must be emphasised here that the protagonist's attainment of self cannot be realized fully in the present time frame. When he finally leaves London to return to Malaya, he realizes that the life awaiting him in his homeland would also affect the identity and sense of self he forms in London. This realization is reflective of the evolving identity of the migratory individual. It also enhances the notion that the identity is constantly reconstituted and is in continuous flux. Thus, it must be emphasised here that the life awaiting the migrant in his homeland could affect the identity and sense of self he forms in the host society.

The sections above have discussed the psychological perspectives towards the protagonist's identity and sense of self under transcultural circumstances. The aspects of culture, race, gender and sexual orientation are used in the analysis of the protagonist's negotiation of identity and sense of self. It can be concluded that not all psychological perspectives were applicable to the analysis.

POSTCOLONIAL PERSPECTIVES TO IDENTITY AND SENSE OF SELF IN TRANSCULTURAL EXPERIENCES

This section will contain an analysis of the protagonist's negotiation of identity and sense of self using postcolonial perspectives. Elements of the postcolonial approach that will be used are displacement, alienation/marginalization, othering and assimilation. These elements will be analysed based on culture, race, gender and sexual orientation based on the protagonist's speech, thought, and actions in the novel.

DISPLACEMENT AND TRANSCULTURAL EXPERIENCES

This section will analyse the sense of displacement in the protagonist from a culture and country that is new to him. Displacement is also referred to as dislocation. Displacement occurs as a result of imperial occupation and the experiences associated with this event. This phenomenon, according to Ashcroft, Griffiths and Tiffin,

> may be a result of transportation from one country
> to another by slavery or imprisonment, by invasion
> and settlement, a consequence of willing or unwilling
> movement from a known location to an unknown

location. The term is used to describe the experiences of those who have willingly moved from the imperial home to the colonial margin.

(1998: 73)

Displacement is often described using the terms 'unhousedness' or 'not-at-home-ness'. This term was coined by Heidegger (Ashcroft, Griffiths and Tiffin: 1998). Displacement occurs in many forms. Among them include, physical, emotional, gender, cultural, sexual, racial, political and social displacement. However, this research will only be limited to four areas, namely culture, race, gender and sexual orientation.

CULTURE AND DISPLACEMENT

The protagonist's negotiation of his identity and sense of self through culture is seen in his encounters with the host culture as well as interactions and relationships with the other characters he comes into contact with. The protagonist's encounters with the colonizing culture are seen to cause conflict between his Malayan Chinese experiences and the transcultural experiences he delves upon in London.

The research shows that the protagonist experiences cultural displacement from the host culture as well as the homeland culture. As an individual who has experienced colonialism, the protagonist is highly diverse in nature and his traditions. As a being in two cultures, his sense of identity and self is constantly under construction and change. This change will inevitably lead him to feel a sense of displacement from his homeland as well as the host society.

The protagonist's cultural displacement is detected when Cordelia asks him his opinion of girls being accosted by males. When posed with such a question, the protagonist automatically recalls the manner in which women in his country are treated by the males. When he realizes that he seems to be from a culture *where fathers were adulterous and mothers vicious and a river of lies poured itself between them separating* (pg 18), the protagonist feels that he is not able to give Cordelia a definite reply. This is because the protagonist feels that he comes from a culture where communication between a man and woman is not always truthful. The protagonist is aware that the Asian culture sees occurrence of extra-marital affairs as a supplement to a marriage, leading to the degrading of the female. Nevertheless, the female has to uphold her family name in an attempt to save the face of the husband and the family. Thus, when Cordelia asks the protagonist for his opinion, he feels unable to be truthful. The examples above indicate that the protagonist is in conflict with the culture of his homeland as well as the culture of the host society. It is felt that the protagonist's displacement in terms of the culture of his homeland and the culture of the host society prompts him to shift into a hybrid space.

The protagonist's feeling of displacement is also observed when he says *But now this girl was forcing me to give an answer about something I would have discussed frankly only with men* (pg 18). This feeling of displacement stems off the reasoning of his homeland culture that certain sensitive topics should only be discussed with individuals of the same gender. Nevertheless, the protagonist takes her question in good spirit and looks at it as a means of strengthening their relationship. This is evident when he says, *And so, in smoothing the way, I created my first creek with her* (pg 18).

In the situation above, the cultural displacement faced by the protagonist is apparent in his social encounters with women of the host society. The protagonist also finds it difficult to comprehend the host society's social custom where marriage is deemed unnecessary in a relationship. This custom differed vastly from the customs of his home culture which stipulates that marriage was imminent when one is in a relationship or when one reaches marriageable age. The protagonist's negotiation of cultural displacement can also be seen in the problems he has with the English language. It was found that the protagonist's lack of proficiency in the English language often leaves him feeling confused and self-conscious. Although he embraces inadequacies, he often regrets the fact that he cannot speak as fluently as his expatriate counterparts. The protagonist wishes how he can . . .

> . . . only say wonderful nonsensical things as they did, lightly with grace; but when I talked my words became inconsequential, losing their force, and as I spoke I became conscious of my pronunciation. Marbles in my mouth: I spewed them out. I hated myself as soon as I began to speak, feeling inadequate . . . (pg 25).

For the protagonist, the English language was the only means through which he could converse with his friends. The difficulty he faces in communicating his feelings and ideas to his friends devastates him and stirs feelings of despair in him.

When the protagonist attends a party hosted by Tristam, he once again feels a sense of displacement when he finds that the efforts he puts to identify himself with the western crowd seems fruitless. According to the protagonist, *Although I had opened up my pores drinking in everything I could from these new civilisations, remoulding my mind, so much so that I carried on conversations in my head in their language, I neither felt, however much I tried, their anger nor their pity, their worry nor their intensity* (pg 55). The protagonist later suppresses his feeling of displacement with beer and ends up making a mockery of himself by getting drunk. It is felt that the protagonist's suppression of his feelings could have been caused by the unexamined identity development stage. This stage makes him lack the desire to look into his identity and reconstitute it. From the perspective of the social identity theory, his behaviour could have been prompted by his actions of isolating himself from the host society after being rejected by Cordelia.

At this stage, the protagonist's individual identity is defined by the collective identity he assumes when he is in interaction with the receiving society. The damage to his collective identity is apparent when he is rejected by the subculture within the host society, as represented by Cordelia. This rejection affects his individual identity and causes him to isolate himself from the receiving/host society.

This feeling of isolation becomes a reason behind the crisis of identity he faces. This crisis of identity is a result of the pressure he faces in his attempts at internalizing the role he is expected to play in the host society. It is felt that he is unable to play this role well due to the changing nature of the host society in accepting and defining the protagonist's migrant role in the receiving society. This changing nature of the receiving society then influences the protagonist by unconsciously imposing the notion that the migrant is 'other'. This feeling of being othered sends the protagonist into a process of self-interaction, which in turn makes him mediate his own identity. The mediation of his own identity prompts him to isolate himself when he faces a sense of rejection from the host society.

RACE AND DISPLACEMENT

With regards to the element of race and displacement, it has been observed that the protagonist's negotiation of racial identity in transcultural contexts affects his interactions with the members of Tristam's League of Coloured People club. The protagonist's association with the club is seen when he accompanies Tristam to a meeting session, although he is not overly enthusiastic or excited about the meeting. Tristam compels him to come along so he (the protagonist) can get acquainted with the members of the club. Although the protagonist is received warmly at the meeting, he feels a slight sense of displacement due to his oriental looks. The protagonist's sense of displacement is highlighted when he gets a curious look from a reverend who attends the meeting as well. The protagonist's discomfort is described in the following sentence: *Rev Barker was busy shaking hands with us, looking at us with interest* (pg 147). The protagonist feels that Rev. Barker's interest in them (the protagonist and Gopal) is not of genuine interest but out of curiosity. It is felt that Rev. Barker's inquisitiveness is symbolic of the coloniser's attraction to the exotic nature of the colonised.

However, the sense of racial displacement the protagonist feels takes a turn when Derek and Guy, who accompany the protagonist, Gopal and Tristam to the meeting are viewed as strangers by the expatriate members of the League of Coloured People. Instead of being looked upon as a symbol of colonial supremacy (as they are Westerners), Derek and Guy are subjected to 'curious glances' (pg144) by members of the club. Feeling out of place, *Derek and Guy sat in the shadows, kept very quiet, accepting curious glances flung at them* (pg 144). The displacement of Derek and Guy can be explained using Tajfel and Turner's (1986) concept of categorisation and identification from the social identity theory. The concept of categorisation explains that we categorise people in order to understand the social environment. This concept is helpful because if we can assign people to a category, then that tells us something about the people who have been grouped. Identification allows the individual to identify with groups that they see themselves belonging to. The behaviour of the members of the club therefore is an act of categorisation because they have categorised Derek and Guy into the grouping of British subjects and not into the grouping of the expatriate community. The categorization of Derek and Guy imply that the members of the club acknowledge them as the colonizing force and not as members of their expatriate in-group. The perception of the club members of Derek and Guy as colonial figures, encourage them (the club members) to displace Derek and Guy as they do not identify with Derek and Guy as members of their (the club members) in-group.

The situation highlighted in the example above reflects that people are discriminated because of the way they appear to other individual's. The natives are treated in an indifferent manner because they are deemed inferior to the immigrants. As a result, characters like the protagonist and Gopal are seen as individuals who are not worthy of any respect as they are of second class status. But this situation is twofold. This is because white people are also discriminated against by the non-whites. Although Derek and Guy are not British, they are differentiated by the non-whites due to the colour of their skin and their racial background. The racial displacement highlighted in the situations above has been described using the concept of categorisation from the social identity theory. The act of categorizing individuals is a method of isolation. The act of isolating an individual could be risky as these individuals could resist the stereotypes they have been cast in.

GENDER AND DISPLACEMENT

The protagonist's sense of displacement is also apparent in terms of gender. His sense of displacement is mostly seen in the manner in which he feels displaced when he interacts with individuals of his own sex. Gender displacement is observed when the protagonist socializes with his gay friends. An example of the protagonist's sense of discomfort is projected in the following statement he makes, *I hastily replied, 'Oh, but it's not mine. Tristam lent it to me'. Guy smiled quietly and this made me more embarrassed* (pg 124). The protagonist's hasty reply makes Guy smile. Upon seeing Guy smile, the protagonist feels more embarrassed. The protagonist's hasty reply and embarrassed state is reflective of his discomfort in addressing the issue of homosexuality. More importantly, the protagonist does not want to be classified as a homosexual himself. This fear results in his resistance of the norms of the host culture that promotes homosexuality as a way of life and alignment with the culture of his homeland that disapproves of such practices. The protagonist's actions indicate that his identity and sense of self is still moulded by homeland culture. The protagonist feels that in the Asian culture, homosexuality is unacceptable and individuals who were of this nature were ostracised and alienated from the community and society at large. Thus, it is of no surprise that the protagonist feels displaced.

As the protagonist's friendships with his gay friends become stronger, he starts to develop an understanding and sympathy for his friends. This understanding is suggestive of the in-group identification process advocated by the social identity theory. So, when Tristam tries to seduce him, the protagonist takes his advances without much seriousness. In a similar attempt towards the protagonist by Steve, the protagonist once again avoids the sexual advances of his gay friend by kindly explaining that his irrationality is a product of his drunkenness. Here, the protagonist demonstrates a strong sense of self as he is able to maintain a firm stand on his own sexuality. Although he is tempted by new sexual experiences, he does not give in to the urges of his friends, even if it is for the sake of experimentation.

It is felt that Tristam and Steve are sexual colonisers. This is evident in this extract in which the narrator repositions Tristam's role from a scrounger to invader. At the same time, the protagonist is reinforcing his own position as an innocent victim.

On first noticing him, I remained very still in my bed and focused my gaze on the top of his head; my hands became tensed under the sheets. My expression must have been blank; I had the same feeling that I experienced as a child when I lay in bed looking at an eight-legged spider moving across the ceiling (pg 237).

The protagonist perceives Tristam's and Steve's sexual advances as menacing but is nonetheless drawn to sympathise with them. He begins to understand that his gay friends are like other human beings with needs. This appreciation leads him to accept and value his friends and understand the nature of homosexuality. The protagonist's feelings of displacement with regards to homosexuality are seen to evolve from a negative perspective to a positive one. This change of perception could be a possible outcome of the protagonist's successful control of his ability to conform and integrate with the host society. This ability indicates that the protagonist is able to derive a positive self-concept from his personal (individual) and social (collective) identity. This positive self-concept in turn helps him identify himself as a part of the host community.

SEXUAL ORIENTATION AND DISPLACEMENT

It can be concluded that no explicit indication of sexual displacement in clearly apparent in the text. The protagonist's heterosexual sexual encounters provide him with experiences that are new to him, to which he adapts without much difficulty to relationships with Cordelia and Beatrice except for his escapades with homosexuality.

The protagonist's sense of displacement is apparent from cultural, racial, and gender aspects. Nevertheless, the protagonist is seen to accept certain norms of the colonizing power. This acceptance is seen particularly in matters pertaining to gender and sexual orientation.

His acceptance of certain norms of the host society indicates that the protagonist repositions his identity and sense of self under transcultural circumstances both consciously and unconsciously.

ALIENATION/MARGINALIZATION AND TRANSCULTURAL EXPERIENCES

In his course of negotiating his identity and sense of self under transcultural circumstances, the protagonist faces alienation and marginalization. Not only is he alienated by the culture of the host society (London), the protagonist is also alienated as a result of differences in race and sexual orientation. In addition to being alienated, there are a few instances in the novel that suggest that the protagonist alienates or distances himself from the people and culture of the host culture. These instances will be investigated in the following sections.

CULTURE AND ALIENATION/MARGINALIZATION

The protagonist's cultural alienation is found in the prologue of the novel:

> Two milk bottles stood on the table—one full, the other three quarters full—and spreading out beneath them *The Times* lay prostrate, its columns dirtied with the spilt contents of chilli sauces and mashed pickled prawns that dripped from the abandoned bottles and vials. At one corner, a small bowl balanced on the edge, its leafy green surface tarnished with gluey remains. This was my dining table, a littered no-man's land. The opened can, quarter full, its bright purple wrapper torn, gave out a rich smell. What was it she had said, as she scooped out the lychee, balancing the fruit on the tip of her forefinger? 'Flesh pink' with a laugh, as she rested her hand against her bare throat.

*London was full of rooms. I went from one to the other.
Slowly I adjusted myself and lived the life of a troglodyte,
learning the tribal customs of feints and apologies. And
sitting with my back to the brown wall paper, on the
narrow bed, I looked across the small room, through
the pale patch of the window, dreaming of mynah birds
shooting like beads along branches of casuarinas, and of
pale spidery crabs on warm sands and the dark button-
sized shells buried just above the tides. With my mouth
opened against the crumpled pillow, after she left, I
listened to the hollow breathing that filled my lungs
and the two cords of muscles along my spine tensed
with regrets, watching heavy-lidded, how my forefinger
twitched forlornly. And a few phrases came to my mind.
Once she had written Understand—and your heart can be
mother to all things—I have found a big red tomato this
afternoon—soft and full of silky dreams.*

*Solitary like a spider, weaving a web, I had written to her.
Not of love, because we did not speak of love. But of what
I had dreamt, awkwardly framing the words, with the
concentration of a child filling in his first notebook, intent
to please, and words became my courage and her tribute.
Not about the past either; for in this city, men and women
submerged their past. I swam along with them, flipping my
fins* (pg 9-10).

The excerpt above describes the place the protagonist stays at in
London. The protagonist's description of his confined living quarters,
and the surrounding city of London, is expressive of his sense of
alienation and negativity of the 'centre'. His table is a *littered no-
man's land*. Reference to this room is also made in Chapter Six of the
novel, where Tristam describes the room as a mausoleum. It is felt
that the mausoleum is reflective of protagonist's burial of his Malayan
individuality and distinctness, in his preparation for his reception of
British values.

In the extract, London is described in ancient and profound terms. For example, he lives the life of a *troglodyte*, moving from one room to another, taking on the *tribal customs of feints and apologies.* The act of the protagonist shifting from one room to another foregrounds his immigrant nature. The protagonist's use of words like 'abandoned', 'small' and 'pale' are reflective of his alienated feelings and emotions. The sentence *At one corner, a small bowl balanced on the edge, its leafy green surface tarnished with gluey remains*, is symbolic of the protagonist's situation in London. Describing himself as a 'bowl balanced on the edge', the protagonist symbolically indicates that his life as a migrant in the host society is as unstable and insecure as the bowl balancing its self on the edge of the table.

Contrasted against this description of London is the memory of his homeland, Malaya. The protagonist describes Malaya in vibrant terms. Malaya is described by the protagonist with a sense of warmth and affection, in contrast to the overpowering desolation of his present life in London. He dreams of the mynah birds of his home country but can only continue to exist as a cave-dweller in London. His descriptions are distinctly in contrast with perceptions of the host society as the rescuer and liberator of humanity. This provides an ironic inversion of the colonial power as the caretaker and provider to her colonial subjects.

In addition to being alienated, the protagonist is also seen to alienate himself. Two instances in which the protagonist alienates himself have been found. The first example deals with the protagonist's opinion of Tristam's conversational skills. The protagonist feels that Tristam does not seem to possess the ability to express his views and opinions in a direct manner. The protagonist is of the opinion that Tristam is very 'abstract' (pg 131) when he explains certain matters. According to the protagonist, Tristam,

> did not have the facility of placing his finger on the point
> and had to go around in a circle, expounding the periphery
> of the central idea. Whether he was talking about racial
> relations or friendship, his concern did not communicate
> itself. Instead I was left with a feeling that he was building

> a brittle shell where all his precious ideas remained hidden
> (pg 131).

Instead of paying intent attention to Tristam, the protagonist closes his eyes, does not reply and waits for Tristam to continue with his conversation. The protagonist's silent approach is reflective of the protagonist alienating himself from the conversation he has with Tristam. Not wanting to hurt Tristam's feelings, the protagonist keeps himself voiceless.

The protagonist's actions are symbolic of the process of resistance, which is advocated by Fanon in his evolutionary scheme of the coloniser-colonised relationship. Although the protagonist does not resist Tristam vocally, the protagonist applies silent resistance on him. This technique appears to work well for the protagonist as Tristam suddenly becomes nervous of carrying on with his conversation with the protagonist and eventually turns his face away from him. In the second situation, the protagonist reflects upon Tristam's lessons on proper behavioural etiquette.

> Sometimes Tristam questioned my attitude. 'You're very formal,' Tristam once said to me, 'but life is not. That'll be your tragedy. And you hold yourself back too much'. I accepted his verdict in silence as at that moment, I felt very tired and did not want to engage myself in one of those long conversations which Tristam seemed to thrive on (pg 138).

The protagonist is aware that there is a certain degree of truth to Tristam's views. Unable to tolerate Tristam's lessons of life, the protagonist seems to alienate himself from Tristam. The protagonist does this by accepting Tristam's comments of him without much protest because the protagonist does not want to *engage myself* (himself) *in one of those long conversations which Tristam seemed to thrive on*. The protagonist is not the only person to be a beneficiary of the 'astuteness' of Tristam. In addition to the protagonist, Tristam also imparts his worldly knowledge on other characters, especially Gopal, a member of the League of Coloured People. Tristam's comments of Gopal are rather offensive. This could be due to the fact that Tristam takes Gopal under his wings with the hopes of making Gopal more attuned to the British way of life. For instance, Tristam says of Gopal,

> *Gopal's really warm inside. If he could only uncoil himself. You know, funnily enough, his greatest immediate problem is women. He's so shy of them and yet he wants them desperately. I don't know much about his background, but I can't see why he just wouldn't go out and grab one* (pg 145).

However, Gopal is not able to resist and survive the pressure forced onto him by Tristam. Gopal eventually turns mad and is sent to the asylum. In his state of madness, Gopal blames Tristam for pressurizing him. This is evident when Gopal says, *Scold. Scold. When I want girls, scold. When I want girls. Scold* (pg 175). Gopal's situation can be described using the social identity theory. According to this theory, individuals who feel the least welcome in a society new to them will retain a sense of otherness. This sense of otherness will permeate their concept of self and may lead the migrant to develop a negative sense of self. A similar predicament is faced by Gopal. The negative concept of self in Gopal strengthens his sense of self. This strong sense of self makes it difficult for him to conform and assimilate with the norms and culture of the host society, hence turning him mad.

Tristam's attitude is typical of the coloniser who imposes his systems of value over the colonised. Being aware that he could not throw his weight around his British friends for the fear of being ridiculed, Tristam feels the need to exert his power over his expatriate friends, especially his Asian friends.

It must nevertheless be emphasised that the situation is rather ironic. Although Tristam means well when he offers the protagonist advice to be more informal and interact more with people around him, the truth of the situation is that Tristam himself needs guidance pertaining to his personal life. His flaws are aptly described by Steve, Tristam's partner.

Tristam is a fine chap but there can be too much of him. He tends to dominate and is a hell of a sticky person. Not to say I don't like him. I like him a lot. But he wears his grievances on his sleeve and wants everything his way. Very curious about people. Probably that's why he called on you (pg 227).

It has been observed from the research that the West has the power to make the migrant individual see and experience themselves as the 'other'. In LDNBTM, the power of the West is symbolised by Tristam. Tristam is seen to misuse his status as a colonizing figure to alienate the protagonist from the host society. As he has been defined as alien and 'other', the protagonist is compelled to undergo a change in role expectations and status. He must then reconsider his self in a reflexive process as he has encountered the culture and norms of the host society.

RACE AND ALIENATION/MARGINALIZATION

The protagonist's alienation/marginalization in terms of race is observed when he is stared at because of his oriental appearance. The protagonist's sense of alienation is seen one particular day when he and Guy are on their way to a meeting of the League of Coloured People. As they walk, the protagonist notices a British couple-the woman crying and the man pretending not to notice that she is sobbing. As the couple pass them, the man *suddenly turned and glared* (pg 141) at the protagonist. The man's *unexpected* and *concentrated* look makes the protagonist feel uncomfortable. The actions of the man make the protagonist feel degraded, marginalised and disrespected. The actions of the couple can be analysed from the perspective of the social identity theory, specifically the process of identification. The identification process advocates that the individual will identify people or groups they see themselves belonging to. Thus, when the couple come across the protagonist, they consciously alienate him as he does not belong to the host society they identify themselves with.

When the protagonist attends the meeting of the League of Coloured People, he feels as an outsider and alienated when Tristam uses him and Gopal as 'guinea pigs' (pg 145) to make his meeting more eventful. Although Tristam feels that putting the protagonist and Gopal on show would be helpful to the aims of his club, he does not realise that he is indirectly alienating the protagonist and Gopal. The protagonist also feels alienated when he discovers that his Asian physique is not as appealing as that of the white male. This is evident when he says *His clothes sat so well on his frame, mine hung from me as though they were the cast-offs from some elder brother* (pg 230) as he observes Steve. The protagonist unconsciously weakens his own self-worth and sense of self when he compares himself to the white male.

SEXUAL ORIENTATION AND ALIENATION/MARGINALIZATION

The protagonist's alienation in terms of sexual orientation is observed when he distances himself from Beatrice after having intimate relations with her. However, his effort at avoiding Beatrice proves ineffective. Instead of alienating himself from her, he finds himself drawn to her even more. From the analysis, it has been detected that the alienation and marginalization faced by the protagonist is at times self-inflicted. The protagonist alienates himself from people because he does not want to hurt their feelings or make them feel insignificant. The protagonist's act of alienating himself is reflective of his rejection of certain norms and beliefs of the host society. On the other hand, the alienation he is faced with creates a sense of isolation in the protagonist. According to the social identity theory, this feeling of isolation creates a marginalised identity and sense of self in the individual.

Noteworthy in the novel is that the protagonist's name is never revealed. The author, Lee Kok Liang goes to great lengths to keep the protagonist's name hidden from the reader. The action of not revealing the name of the protagonist reflects the trauma of the protagonist in an environment alien to him. This act is also representative of the act of self-alienation. The suppression of the protagonist's name is also indicative of his bruised sense of self. It could also symbolize the assertion that all immigrants are confronted with similar traumas.

OTHERING AND TRANSCULTURAL EXPERIENCES

The protagonist in the novel LDNBTM is also subjected to the phenomenon of othering. Othering describes the various ways in which colonial discourse produces its subjects. The colonised subject is characterised as 'other' while the colonizing master is characterised as 'Other'. According to Ashcroft, Griffiths and Tiffin (1998), the 'other' is described as those who are marginalized by imperial discourse and are identified by their difference from the host culture.

CULTURE AND OTHERING

The protagonist's othering in terms of culture is detected from his level of proficiency of the English language. This is noticed when the protagonist attends a party hosted by Tristam. The protagonist is othered by Ken (a friend of Beatrice) when he speaks to Beatrice. The othering of the protagonist is obvious when he realises: *He* (Ken) *was deliberately embarrassing me before Beatrice, speaking a language with her that I could never master* (pg 63).

The protagonist also feels othered when he is labelled as an *intriguing person* (pg 69) by Tristam and Steve. Their observation of the protagonist is typical of the colonizing 'Other' who feels that he is more superior to the 'other'. Although the protagonist tries to defend himself by denying their definition of him as being intriguing, his efforts prove unsuccessful. It is felt that the protagonist tries to defend himself because he wants to prove to them that he has assimilated with the culture of the host society. However, it is felt that his behaviour indicates that he is in denial. The protagonist's actions could be because he feels that his sense of self is being threatened.

The protagonist's feeling of being othered is sensed yet again when he pays Beatrice a visit. When the protagonist arrives at Beatrice's house,

Ken also arrives minutes later. While talking, Ken suddenly brings up the issue of the protagonist tearing down the curtains during the party at Tristam's house. The protagonist feels othered when Ken attacks him in a blunt manner and with the intent of embarrassing him due to the fact that the protagonist was not used to the directness of westerners when they communicate with each other. Hence, the protagonist feels othered by Ken's action. Here, the clash of cultural norms and the lack of tolerance lead to othering.

RACE AND OTHERING

The protagonist also faces the phenomenon of othering because he is of Asian origin. Although his close friends do not 'other' him intentionally, there are certain instances in which the protagonist feels 'othered' as a result of the actions or comments of his friends.

The protagonist's sense of othering is observed when he is cast aside by a white woman when he patronizes a shop for some chicken noodle soup. When the protagonist absent-mindedly pushes his hand over the counter to make his payment, he does not realise that he has offended her for trying to make his payment first. Unsatisfied with the forwardness of the protagonist, she *threw the protagonist a glance as if to say 'Get out of my way'* (pg 142). In another situation, Tristam exploits the protagonist's oriental appearance to promote the aims of his (Tristam's) club. Tristam's action generates a sense of othering in the protagonist.

In another situation, the protagonist is othered by Dickie, Arlette's boyfriend. When the protagonist is introduced to Dickie for the first time, he is deemed as an object instead of a living being. This is evident when Dickie says, *Hullo? What have we got here? Introductions, please'* (pg 42). Dickie's proud behaviour and authority of being a representative figure of the Other is also evident in the following extract, *Like most Englishmen, Dickie, I noticed, believed it much safer to talk about foreigners and politics to strange looking persons. Once I caught Dickie looking at me intently for a few seconds, his eyes glazed like those of a fish.* (pg 44)

GENDER AND OTHERING

In terms of gender, the protagonist is othered by the white women who attend Tristam's party. Wanting to be a well-mannered party guest, the protagonist introduces himself to the guests at the party. Although the protagonist receives a positive response from the men, he is not so lucky with the women. This is evident when the protagonist realises that *the men lifted their hunches when I held their hands, but the women flung up their bright faces and then lost interest in me* (pg 52). The protagonist feels intimidated when he is treated in such a manner. However, he does not voice his dissatisfaction. The protagonist's actions indicate that his identity and sense of self is at the stage of conformity that is he is in the phase of assimilating the norms of the dominant host culture. It is felt that the protagonist's conformity is a result of him wanting to preserve his collective identity rather than his individual identity.

The analysis shows that the othering of the protagonist takes place from the aspect of culture, race and gender. However, the protagonist does not face the phenomenon of othering from the aspect of sexual orientation. Ironically, the othering he is subjected to makes him a braver and stronger person emotionally and psychologically. This positive attitude of the protagonist which develops from his transcultural experiences in London helps him better negotiate the challenges he is confronted with.

ASSIMILATION AND TRANSCULTURAL EXPERIENCES

Even though the protagonist is displaced, othered and alienated, he still takes the extra effort to assimilate with the host society. The protagonist's assimilation with the host society indicates that he tries to select and invent from the culture of the host society to assist him with his negotiation of his evolving identity and sense of self. The protagonist's effort at assimilation not always proves successful. The analysis below indicates this.

Culture and Assimilation

The protagonist tries to assimilate with the culture of the host society in certain ways. His efforts at assimilation are seen in his attempt to identify with the mainstream society (the host culture) and expatriate subculture within the society. His efforts at blending in with the crowd in seen when he places importance on the manner he dresses.

> *I smiled, growing warm under the new red polo sweater I bought a week ago. I had put it on trembling and stood before the mirror; dissatisfied, I took it off and flung it on the bed. But it lay like a challenge; so I wore it again and quickly slipped on my jacket in case I should change my mind. Usually I choose greys to wear, not daring any of the cockatoo colours, but then Tristam came one day and looked over my clothes and started to persuade me to try something bright for a change (pg 103).*

The protagonist's effort at blending in with the host society is apparent when he chooses to wear dark coloured attire. It is felt that his preference for dark coloured outfits is caused by his reluctance of wanting to be conspicuous in the host society. This could be because the protagonist does not want to make his efforts at integrating with the host society more complicated. However, when Tristam persuades him to wear bright attire for a change, the protagonist accepts Tristam's idea. According to the social identity theory, if and when a particular group identity becomes salient at a particular time the sentiments, emotions and behaviours of any given member of the salient group will tend to be affected and guided by the norms and aspirations of that group. Thus, the protagonist's action of choosing to wear bright attire is actually guided by the values and hopes of the members of his in-group. The protagonist accepts the advice of his group members in order to satisfy the expectations of his group. It is felt that the protagonist puts in enormous effort at assimilating with the host society as he wants the members of the subculture community within the host society to accept him and have a positive view of him. This positive view of him would give him an advantage in the long run as it would not only lead the host society to present him with preferential treatment but would also enable him to boost his self-esteem. This in turn would help him achieve a positive sense of self from his transcultural encounters.

The protagonist's actions of putting the sweater on and then taking it off and later wearing it back again is also symbolic of his indecisiveness in assimilating the culture of the host society. But when Tristam advices him *to try something bright for a change*, the protagonist decides to change his sombre clothes for brighter ones. The protagonist's effort at assimilation with the host culture is also noticed in the following situation: I *opened my mouth to cry out, but like an alarm my mind sent out a warning message. In this country, no-one cried out, even though they might be dying* (pg 117). The situation above takes place when the protagonist tries to chase a shadowy figure, whom he thinks is Cordelia. Wanting to shout out to the figure to stop, the protagonist realises that such an action would be deemed rude behaviour in the culture of the coloniser. Thus, he does not call out for her although he is aware that he could be missing out on his chance of finally being able to locate her.

It is apparent that the protagonist's attempts at assimilating and adapting to the culture and practices of the receiving society can be seen as positive, enriching, dynamic and at the same time oppressive. This positive and negative confrontation could cause the protagonist to experience an unstable development of identity.

SEXUAL ORIENTATION AND ASSIMILATION

In terms of sexual orientation, the protagonist does not seem to have any trouble acculturing himself with the sexual conducts of the host society. The protagonist's sexual encounters with Cordelia and Beatrice create new experiences for him. These experiences are those which the protagonist never had the opportunity to encounter in his homeland.

For instance, the protagonist is exposed to the notion of premarital sexual relations and the freedom of not having to marry a woman although he has a relationship with her. Although the protagonist comes from a culture that forbids such acts he takes liberty to break the rules imposed by his home culture. Being away from his homeland gives the protagonist the freedom to engage in such acts. The protagonist seizes these opportunities without reservation. The protagonist's act can be explained using the social identity theory. This theory explains that when the individual changes geographic places, he enters a different social space in which new ties, symbols, objects and situations are encountered. The individual must then reconsider his concept of self in his attempts at assimilating with the receiving society. So, when the protagonist is confronted with sexual experiences he could never encounter in Malaya, he makes use of the opportunity presented to him. Thus, it can be concluded that the protagonist's geographic location gives him the freedom to experience new sexual exposures without reservation.

The loss of Cordelia creates an awareness of the superficiality of his sense of self. He says, *What was real and meaningful to me remained hidden and submerged, festering in the dark like an abscess, giving me continuous twinges of pain and discomfort* (pg 229). Not only is the protagonist's statement reflective of his doomed relationship with Cordelia, it is also symbolic of the protagonist's difficulties in coming to terms with his identity and sense of self. This statement is proof that the protagonist is confused and is still in search of his 'true' identity.

His brief journey to Paris also makes him a more mature person. He returns from his journey to Paris, a new man. Upon his return, the protagonist cleans his room instead of calling on his friends. This is evident in the following excerpt:

> *It rained the week after I had returned to London. Two layers of sound; the crisp crackling like popcorns bursting on my window ledge, and the background of humming, droning, the rise and fall of the wind, of the rain falling into the courtyard below. I had not rung up Ken or Beatrice or Tristam for the past week, preferring them to think that I was still in Paris. Instead, I tidied up my room, moving methodically through the wasteland* (pg 223).

The protagonist's act of cleaning the 'wasteland' in his room is symbolic of his renewal and repositioning of identity and sense of self. This act appears to be the discarding of his old self to usher in a more enlightened self.

> . . . *I congratulated myself that I was not so naïve as to accept that explanation at face value. I had become cynical about such things, looking for angles all the time. To me, self-interest was the genuine touchstone of everyone's action. I had discarded my old habit of thought which treated everyone as Christ like figures* (pg 229).

The protagonist's repositioned self is evident in the manner he makes judgements of people. He is no longer the person who *could never bring myself* (himself) *to challenge the opinion of anyone* (pg 81). It is also observed that his actions of 'cleansing himself' of his old self are conscious efforts.

Cordelia's departure leads him to become closer to Beatrice. The friendship he has with Beatrice later turns into love. Beatrice also helps him understand his evolving identity and sense of self. The protagonist's re-identification with his homeland self in transcultural circumstances is reflective of the notion of transnationalism advocated by the social identity theory. The extract below supports this point:

> *Should I also tell her about the dirt and the flies and the diseases? However, what is the point anyway? Everyone of us must preserve a certain romantic viewpoint about far distant places to which the mind could return in the midst of our grimy surroundings or when life pressed too harshly upon our individual existence. She would, I had hoped, always associate the glitter and the shadow with me and when I had gone, perhaps on some wintry morning when she looked out from her window at the dull soft-drizzling sky and the dark street, she would think of me walking slowly, my long shadow falling before me, carefully dressed in white, along a dry street that burned like a salt mine.*

> *And I on my part would recapture the glitter in her eyes*
> *sitting in the dark of a cinema hall, her coat unbuttoned,*
> *breathing gently by my side with the tips of her fingers*
> *resting coldly on my palm. I was conscious that I was a*
> *craftsman, weaving on the loom of memory, sending out*
> *a rhythm that would enfold our lives like the caresses of*
> *waves on a sandy beach* (pg 248).

As the time for the author's return to his Malayan homeland draws near, the protagonist grapples with the disillusionment of his European experience. Cordelia and London are already dead to him. Memories of London and Cordelia are now irreconcilable with the memories of his homeland. The protagonist is seen to progress towards an understanding of the problematic colonial experience and ultimately a justification of his identity and sense of self. This is evident when he says,

> *And I lay quietly for the ache to return, fearfully but with*
> *gladness, like a sick person counting the hours when the*
> *next attack would come so that his lying in wait would*
> *not prove abortive. And therefore I immured myself in*
> *my room, putting order into everything I could lay my*
> *hands on, as I patiently awaited the return of the terrible*
> *feeling that struck me when she left me. In order to*
> *meet her again I had to revive that feeling. Without it,*
> *everything would be such a waste. I might as well be a*
> *puppet, manipulated by her hands, if I did not repossess*
> *my feelings* (pg 224-225).

Through his rejection at the hands of Cordelia and London, the protagonist takes the first tentative steps towards a comprehension of his sense of self. Only in confronting the host society can he move into an unfettered future. In the concluding chapter, the protagonist accepts a gift from Tristam as he boards the train to the airport. The gift Tristam brings is a Norman Collins novel entitled *London Belongs To Me*. This novel provides the ironic twist to LDNBTM. From a Malaysian perspective, the sense of disenchantment that permeates this novel can be seen as liberating. The protagonist's awareness that London does not belong to him is an acknowledgment of the deception of the host culture and the falsity in the search for easy alternatives.

SUMMARY OF FINDINGS

A summary of the findings from the analysis above will be included in this section.

CULTURAL IDENTITY AND SELF

The protagonist's negotiation of his identity and sense of self through the element of culture can be summarised as follows:

- The personal unconscious makes him recall memories of his homeland. The research shows that the protagonist's historical identity is linked to his homeland identity.
- His collective unconscious, which is passed to him by his ancestors disapproves of the female being the hegemonic power in a relationship between a man and a woman. The protagonist's act of rejection of the culture of the host society indicates the stage of separatism in his development of identity. The stage of separatism influences him to reject certain norms of the host society.
- The protagonist's collective unconscious is also embedded with the notion that promiscuous relationships and relationships before marriage is a forbidden act. The protagonist however does not hold fast to this custom of his homeland.
- The protagonist's persona is manifested from his collective unconscious when he hides his true emotions. Pretentiousness and lies are other modes in which his persona functions.
- The protagonist's shadow is seen at play when he manipulates his friends.
- The protagonist's self, embeds a sense of compassion and sympathy in him.

- From a postcolonial perspective, the displacement faced by the protagonist is apparent from his dealings with the host culture and the culture of his homeland. His feeling of displacement in both cultures indicates that his identity exists in a hybrid space.
- As an individual who has experienced colonialism, the protagonist is highly diverse in nature and his traditions. As a being in two cultures, his sense of identity and self is constantly under construction and change.
- Concerning alienation, the protagonist feels alienated from the culture of the host society. Alienation also sparks memories of his homeland. The protagonist is also seen to alienate himself from the host culture.
- The protagonist tries to assimilate with the culture of the host society in certain ways. His efforts at assimilation are seen in his ability to identify with the mainstream society and expatriate subculture within the society. The research shows that the protagonist's attempts at assimilating and adapting to the culture and practices of the receiving society are seen as positive, enriching, dynamic and oppressive.

It can be concluded that the protagonist's negotiation of his evolving identity and sense of self in terms of culture goes through several stages. In terms of the minority development stage, the protagonist's identity seems to develop in the level of conformity. The protagonist's conformity is seen in his internalization of the norms of the host culture. This internalization of norms is seen when he tries to assimilate with the culture of the host society, i.e. in the manner they dress. In terms of the majority identity development stage, the protagonist seems to experience the stages of acceptance and resistance. The protagonist's acceptance is seen in his internalization of the sexual practices of the host culture, for instance the notion of intimate relations before marriage. His resistance is seen in his disapproval of women having a more superior standing instead of men. The protagonist's development of identity in terms of conformity, acceptance and rejection is carried out in a conscious effort. This conscious effort taken by the protagonist indicates that he selects particular elements of the transcultural experiences he is confronted with in order to help him with his negotiation and formation of identity and sense of self. It can be concluded here that the protagonist is still in conflict of identity as he is unable to ascertain his true sense of self. This is because the protagonist still seems to fall back to certain norms of his homeland culture.

RACIAL IDENTITY AND SELF

- The research does not show any indication of the manifestation of the personal unconscious and the persona in the psyche of the protagonist from the perspective of race and psychology.
- The collective unconscious of the protagonist makes him pass judgements about characters of different religion and race. The judgements he makes are from embedded information from his psyche, which are passed onto him from his ancestors.
- The protagonist's shadow manifests ill feelings in him when he is alienated by Tristam during a meeting session of the League of Coloured People. This marginalized feeling is a result of his status as the 'other' in the host society. The research shows that the protagonist's marginalised feeling is a result of this inner compulsion, which compels him to feel marginalized.
- The self-archetype in the protagonist, which emits positive connotations, changes the protagonist's negative perception into a positive perception. This change of perception could be a possible outcome of the protagonist's successful control of his ability to conform and integrate with the host society. This ability indicates that the protagonist is able to derive a positive self-concept from his individual and collective identity. This positive self-concept in turn helps him identify himself as a part of the host community.
- Concerning the element of race and displacement, it has been observed that the protagonist's negotiation of racial identity in transcultural experiences surround his interactions with the members of Tristam's club, the League of Coloured People. Although the protagonist is received warmly at the meeting,

he feels a slight sense of displacement due to his oriental looks.

- The protagonist's alienation/marginalization in terms of race is observed when he is stared at because of the colour of his skin. The protagonist's alienation makes him feel dishonoured, marginalised and insulted. The protagonist also feels alienated when he discovers that his Asian physical make up is not as appealing as the physical make-up of the white male.

The protagonist's identity and sense of self in terms of race seems to be at the unexamined identity level and conformity level of the minority development stage. This is because he accepts the dominant norms of the host culture without making any attempts at assimilation or even rejecting them. His sense of alienation is apparent as he sees himself through the eyes of the host culture. His action of using the culture of the host society as a yardstick to measure his sense of self leaves him feeling inferior to the host culture. This stunts the protagonist's efforts at identity negotiation and formation.

GENDER IDENTITY AND SELF

- There were little indications of the personal unconscious, the collective unconscious and the persona from the perspective of gender at play in the novel.
- The protagonist's manifestation of the shadow however is seen when he mocks Steve and Tristam for being gay. This resistance is reflective of the stage of redefinition in the protagonist's process of identity development.
- In terms of the protagonist's self, the latter does not brush Steve off in a violent manner when he tries to seduce him. The protagonist's laid-back outlook of the situation could have been motivated by the fact that he sympathised with the gay community. The protagonist's courteous, sympathetic and respectful sense of self is a result of the positive qualities embedded in his psyche as well as a growing sense of belief in him. This mounting sense of credence in him is symbolic of the stage of integration in the protagonist's development and

construction of identity. His act of coming to terms with gay practices in the host society indicates that the protagonist is able to assimilate belongingness to the dominant culture.

- His sense of displacement is mostly seen in the manner in which he feels displaced when he addresses the issue of homosexuality. The protagonist's feelings of displacement with regards to homosexuality and his gender are seen to evolve from a negative perspective to a positive one.
- In terms of gender, the protagonist's othering is observed when he is othered by the white women who attend Tristam's party.

In terms of gender, the protagonist's identity development is seen in terms of the majority identity development stage, particularly in terms of redefinition and integration. The protagonist's redefinition of identity is seen in the manner in which he challenges the privilege given to the gay community by the host culture. However, when the protagonist's conception of gays and homosexuality evolve from a negative perception to a positive one, it becomes apparent that the protagonist has integrated with the host culture. This integration indicates that the protagonist is able to assimilate and feel a sense of belonging in the host culture. Thus, the protagonist begins to absorb the culture of the host society. This absorption indicates that he is now able to identify himself with the culture of the host society as well as the culture of his homeland.

SEXUAL IDENTITY AND SELF

- The personal unconscious of the protagonist makes him able to recall memories of his homeland during his secret courtship with Cordelia and later when he has a relationship with Beatrice.
- However, at times, he seems to suppress thoughts of his homeland in an effort not to estrange himself from his thoughts of Malaya. The protagonist's unwillingness to estrange himself from the host culture is symbolic of his trials at assimilating with the host society.

- As the protagonist assumes that he belongs to the in-group of the subculture of the receiving society, he tries to maintain his stand with the host society by suppressing his thoughts of his homeland. This suppression is reflective of him trying to upkeep the sense of identity he has derived thus far as a result of his associations with members of the host society.
- He also seems to reject certain cultural norms in terms of sexual relations that have been passed on to him by his ancestors.
- The persona affects him in a positive manner as well as in a negative manner. The positive outcome of the manifestations of the persona helps the protagonist get along with people. However, the persona encourages him to hide his emotions, lie and pretend to be someone he was not.
- The manifestation of the shadow in the protagonist is perpetrated by his thoughts of losing Cordelia. At a certain point, the protagonist became disoriented and loses his sense of rationality. This loss of rationality is the beginning of manifestation of ill thoughts and actions in the protagonist. The shadow archetype, which manifested in the protagonist, instils negativity in the protagonist. The protagonist became less rational, selfish, neglectful of his own reputation and also negligent of the feelings and emotions of other individuals.
- The protagonist's sense of self instils him with a sense of guilt. This sense of realization of guilt is actually a manifestation of the protagonist's self to rid him off negative emotions. This realization also makes him more optimistic. When the protagonist finally leaves London to return to Malaya, he realizes that the life awaiting him in his homeland would also affect the identity and sense of self he assumes in London.
- There were no explicit indications of displacement in terms of sexual orientation in LDNBTM. This is due to the fact that the protagonist's sexual encounters provide him with experiences, which he never had the opportunity to experience in his homeland. The protagonist's geographic location gives him the freedom to experience new sexual exposures without reservation.

- The protagonist's alienation in terms of sexual orientation is observed when he alienates himself from Beatrice after having a sexual encounter with her. There are also many occasions in which the protagonist practices self-alienation. The protagonist alienates himself from people because he does not want to hurt their feelings or make them feel small. The alienation he is faced with however creates a sense of loneliness in the protagonist.
- In terms of sexual orientation, the protagonist does not seem to have any trouble acculturing himself with the sexual conducts of the host society.

From the analysis, it can be concluded that the protagonist's negotiation of identity and sense of self is seen to be most secure in terms of his sexual orientation. This is due to the fact that the protagonist has the least trouble accepting or rejecting the sexual norms of the host culture. The protagonist's development of identity in terms of the minority and majority identity development stages are represented by the integration stage. As compared to cultural, racial and gender perspectives, the protagonist seems to have developed a secure and confident sexual identity. In addition to integrating the sexual norms of the host culture through his transcultural confrontations, the protagonist is also appreciative of the sexual norms of his homeland culture. In terms of sexual identity, the protagonist does not seem to face many problems in terms of negotiating and forming his identity and sense of self. When he finally leaves London to return to Malaya, he realizes that the life awaiting him in his homeland would also affect the identity and sense of self he forms in London. This realization is reflective of the evolving identity of the migratory individual. It also enhances the notion that the identity is constantly reconstituted and is in continuous flux. Thus, it must be emphasised here that the life awaiting the migrant in his homeland could affect the identity and sense of self he forms in the host society.

The analysis has shown that identity and sense of self is an entity that cannot be fixed or complete. In addition, the finding suggests that the identity of the self in relation to culture, race, gender and sexual orientation are in constant negotiation. When the individual is a migrant, there is a need for him to negotiate his identity and sense of self from the perspective of his homeland culture and the perspective of the host culture. The research shows that migrant individuals are not able to totally disregard the identity of their homeland in their process of negotiating with developments under transcultural circumstances. They embody the identity of a transnational individual. Individuals who embrace transnationalism are able to identify themselves with the culture of the host society as well as the culture of their homeland. The protagonist in LDNBTM is an example of a transnational individual. Upon the individual's return to his homeland, he must be prepared once again to reposition his identity and sense of self. This is because the homeland he left before migration would not be the same homeland he returns to. This renegotiation emphasises that the human identity is always evolving.

CONCLUSION

CHALLENGES OF TRANSCULTURAL OPERATIONS IN THE FORMATION AND REPOSITIONING OF IDENTITY AND SENSE OF SELF OF THE EXPATRIATE INDIVIDUAL

'Transcultural operations involve the selection and invention of materials transmitted by the host culture. This process of selection and invention helps the expatriate individual deal with his identity and sense of self. However, the expatriate individual's identity and sense of self is not a fixed entity. The identity is not fixed as it constantly evolves. This evolution is a result of the individual's negotiation between the identity of his homeland and influences from the transcultural experiences he is confronted with. The transcultural experience is at times used by the expatriate individual to form and reposition his identity and sense of self. This is evident when the individual is already faced with a disillusioned sense of identity and self as a result of his negotiation of identity in the culture of his homeland. However, the expatriate individual must be prepared to face the challenges of transcultural operations in the formation and repositioning of his identity and sense of self. These challenges can be from a psychological perspective and can also be from a societal perspective. These challenges can affect his psychology and can also affect his function and position as an individual in society. The individual must also be prepared to face the consequences of his trials at forming and repositioning his identity and sense of self. Thus, the individual must be ready to face rejection, acceptance and transnationalism' (Sivapalan, 2007: 131).

In the novel, 'the protagonist seems to be a westernized Chinese Malaysian immigrant who migrates to London for a few years to pursue his education. Thinking that the British culture would help him come to terms with his disillusioned homeland identity, the protagonist embarks on and is immersed in transcultural experiences in search of knowledge. The protagonist's transcultural experiences can be viewed in three stages i.e.

- the early stage
- the middle stage
- the final stage

The protagonist's entrance into the transcultural experience represents the early stage. In this stage, the protagonist goes through a sense of confusion. Confusion sets in because the protagonist finds it difficult to adapt to the culture and norms of the British society. This confusion is seen in terms of the cultural, racial, gender and sexual practices of the British. The confusion makes him yearn for his homeland. His yearnings for his homeland are depicted in the form of recollections of Malayan memories. The inability of the protagonist to adapt to the culture of the host society is parallel to Fanon's (1966) description of the native's rejection of the culture of the colonizing force. As the protagonist is a postcolonial individual, he finds it difficult to adjust and relate to the norms of the host culture. For instance, he is unable to comprehend the sexual forwardness of western women and even faces problems with the language of the host culture. As a result of his inability to cope with the culture of the host society, the protagonist feels displaced, alienated and othered from the host society. At this stage, the protagonist's transcultural experience promotes a sense of resistance and separatism from the norms of the host society' (Sivapalan, 2007: 131-132).

'As he begins to confront his sense of confusion, the protagonist gradually moves into the second stage, the middle stage. In the middle stage, the protagonist begins to realise that transcultural experiences can help him with his negotiation of identity and sense of self. His dealing of his sense of confusion is a result of his realization of the positive effects of the transcultural experience towards his continued stay in the environment of the host country. In this stage, the protagonist copies norms of the host country, particularly the sexual norms. For instance, the protagonist copies the norm of having sexual union with women before marriage. He also imitates the host culture in the sense of being intimate with women who have no family ties with him. His actions show that he makes conscious efforts at his adaptation of identity. The protagonist's identity goes through the stage of conformity and acceptance of the host culture in attempt to deal with his feelings of displacement, alienation, marginalization and othering. In essence, he seeks a sense of belonging' (Sivapalan, 2007: 132).

'The third stage represents the period before the protagonist returns home to Malaya. In this stage, the protagonist's identity and sense of self goes through a process of redefinition and integration. The protagonist's redefinition of his identity is seen in his ability to present his views without fear of being criticized by his friends. The protagonist openly voices views and opinions which he once suppressed within him. The protagonist's expression of his views is seen in his ability to contradict certain actions of members of the host culture, with Tristam being the symbolic representation of the host. This is particularly evident in the incident where the protagonist tells Tristam to leave Gopal alone when they visit him in the asylum. Gopal is admitted into the asylum when he turns mad. Gopal's madness is a result of his inability to adapt to the host culture, unlike the protagonist who is able to do so. This makes Gopal completely at odds with the culture of the host country. Gopal's strong sense of self makes it difficult for him to reposition his identity, thus turning him mad. The protagonist however has a stronger sense of rationality. This sense of rationality helps him adapt and reposition his identity for the sake of sanity. Thus, it is noticed that the protagonist's redefinition of identity is done in a conscious effort. The ability of the protagonist to express his views indicates that he begins to develop a secure and confident sense of self' (Sivapalan, 2007: 132-133).

'The protagonist's transcultural experience helps him negotiate his identity and sense of self. The transcultural experience of the protagonist is seen in three phases i.e. the early, middle and final stage. These three stages however pose challenges to the protagonist's formation of identity. Although the protagonist initially succumbs to the pressures of the transcultural experience, he later makes conscious decisions at overcoming the challenges posed by transcultural operations. The protagonist's identity and sense of self thus goes through the stages of resistance and separatism, conformity and acceptance and finally redefinition and integration, particularly from cultural and sexual stages' (Sivapalan, 2007: 133).

RACE, GENDER, CULTURE AND SEXUAL ORIENTATION AS FACTORS SHAPING PERCEPTIONS OF THE SELF

The protagonist's Malaysian cultural experiences and British cultural experiences create conflicting perceptions of selfhood in him. The protagonist's perception of his self and of other characters in terms of culture, race, gender and sexual orientation is seen in his encounters with the British society at large as well as in interactions and relationships with his friends.

CULTURE

The findings show that in terms of culture, the displacement, alienation and othering he faces is instrumental in his perception of his sense of self and the other characters he comes into contact with. The displacement faced by the protagonist is apparent in his social encounters with women and through his lack of competence in the English language. It was found that the protagonist's lack of proficiency in the language of the host country often left him feeling confused and conscious of identity. In terms of his social encounters with women, the protagonist could not comprehend the notion that western women were more outspoken with their views compared to Malaysian women. The alienation of the protagonist is seen in terms of his inability to feel at place with the culture of the host society. The feeling of alienation he experiences evokes memories of his homeland. Being alienated by society, the protagonist also alienates himself from it. This is seen particularly when he isolates himself when in conversations with Tristam. Here, the cultural othering faced by the protagonist is manifested through language use. The protagonist tries to assimilate with the culture of the host society in certain ways. His efforts at assimilation are seen through his ability to identify with the mainstream society and the expatriate subculture within the society. His effort at blending with the crowd is evident when he places importance on his dressing.

RACE

With regards to the element of race and displacement, it has been observed that the protagonist's negotiation of racial identity within transcultural experiences surround his interactions with the members of Tristam's club, the League of Coloured People. Although the protagonist is received warmly at the meeting, he feels a slight sense of displacement due to his oriental looks. The protagonist's alienation/ marginalization is observed when he is stared at because of the colour of his skin. The manner in which the protagonist is estranged makes him feel degraded, marginalised and disrespected. The protagonist also feels alienated when he perceives that his Asian physical make up is not as appealing as the physical make-up of the white male. Therefore, the protagonist faces the phenomenon of othering because of his own consciousness of differences. The protagonist is also othered by white women because they perceive him to be different His perceptions of self and of other characters he comes into contact with are results of his racial sense of difference and is seen in the manner in which he is confronted by displacement, alienation and othering.

GENDER

His sense of displacement with regards to gender is mostly seen in the manner in which he feels out of place when he interacts with individuals of his own sex, as he feels discomfort in addressing the issue of homosexuality. However, as the protagonist's friendships with his gay friends become stronger, he starts to develop a sense of understanding and sympathy for them. The protagonist's feelings of displacement with regards to homosexuality and his gender are seen to progress from a negative perception to a positive one. He also begins to understand that the needs of his gay friends are similar to other human beings. This understanding allows him to conquer his fear of homosexuality.

SEXUAL ORIENTATION

Sexual experiences encountered by the protagonist also help him develop a perception of his self and of other characters he comes into contact with. The protagonist's alienation in terms of sexual orientation is observed when he distances himself from Beatrice after having a sexual encounter with her. There are also many occasions in which he removes himself from sexual encounters. The protagonist alienates himself from people because he does not want to hurt their feelings or make them feel small. His act of distancing is reflective of his rejection of certain norms and beliefs of the host society in repositioning his identity and sense of self under transcultural circumstances. The alienation he is faced with creates a sense of isolation in the protagonist. The protagonist however does not seem to have any trouble acculturing himself with the sexual conducts of the host society. His sexual contacts with Cordelia and Beatrice create new experiences for him. These experiences are that which the protagonist has never had in his homeland.

The findings show culture, race, gender and sexual orientation give the protagonist a positive and negative perception of his sense of self and the other characters he comes into contact with. The positive aspect of culture, race, gender and sexual orientation he is confronted with helps him adapt to the culture of the host country. This in turn helps him reposition his identity and sense of self. When he is confronted with negative aspects of culture, race, gender and sexual orientation, he is seen to take conscious efforts to change these negative perceptions to constructive ones. The effort he puts into this change shows his eagerness to attain a sense of belonging in the host country.

PERSONAL UNCONSCIOUS

'The protagonist's personal unconscious does not help him reveal his feelings for other characters. Instead, the personal unconscious sparks off the protagonist's sense of yearning for his homeland. The yearning for his homeland is manifested in his psyche through his recollection of past events and memories' (Sivapalan, 2007: 133).

COLLECTIVE UNCONSCIOUS

'The protagonist's collective unconscious is embedded with the notion that promiscuity and sex before marriage are a forbidden act. The protagonist however does not adhere to this norm of his homeland. The main reason to this is that the host culture viewed promiscuous behaviour as acceptable. However, the protagonist's collective unconscious also seems to reject the notion that females have hegemonic power in a relationship. As a result, the protagonist at times feels uncomfortable when women appear to take control over his relationship with them. An example of such a woman is Cordelia. Although the protagonist is initially attracted to her, his fascination for her diminishes when she proves to be disloyal and betrays his trust in her. The extension of polite behaviour to other individuals regardless of race and religious beliefs is another element which is embedded within the collective unconscious of the protagonist. The collective unconscious reveals that his politeness could have been influenced by the cultural impact of his homeland' (Sivapalan, 2007: 134).

PERSONA

'The protagonist's persona does not help him reveal his feelings. Instead, the persona helps the protagonist conceal certain feeling and emotions. For instance, he silently struggles with his acquisition of the English language. He also conceals his feeling of alienation when he attends Tristam's party. Pretentiousness and lies are other modes in which the protagonist hides his feelings. This is evident when he pretends to pay interest to Tristam's views on Cocteau and also when he pretends to feel happy when he is with Cordelia. The persona affects him in a constructive manner as well as in a negative one. The positive outcome of the persona helps the protagonist get along with the people around him during his stay in London. However, the persona also affects him in a negative manner as he conceals his emotions and pretends to be someone he is not. These negative manifestations induce the shadow archetype in the psyche of the protagonist' (Sivapalan, 2007: 134).

SHADOW

'The protagonist's shadow is seen at play when he manipulates the feelings and emotions of his friends for his own interest. The shadow in him also compels him to harbour ill feelings towards his friends. The manner in which he secretly ridicules his friends for being gay is also reflective of the evil nature of his shadow. At a certain point, the protagonist became disoriented and irrational. This loss of rationality is the beginning of manifestations of ill thoughts and actions in the protagonist projected by his shadow. A good example of the manifestation of evil and immoral thoughts in the protagonist is seen in his treatment of Beatrice when the shadow perpetrates his thoughts of losing Cordelia. The shadow archetype instils negativity in the protagonist. He became less rational, selfish, neglectful of his own reputation and also negligent of the feelings and emotions of other individuals' (Sivapalan, 2007: 134-135).

SELF

'Some of the actions of the protagonist are motivated by the archetype of self which embeds a sense of compassion and sympathy in him. The self-archetype in the protagonist which emits positive connotations, changes the protagonist's negative perception of his friends into a positive one. The protagonist's sense of self also instils in him with a sense of guilt. His guilty consciousness makes him aware that he treated Beatrice wrongfully on many occasions. His sense of guilt also prompts him to accept Beatrice's love. Beatrice plays an important role in helping the protagonist come to terms with his true sense of self. Although the protagonist feels that Cordelia is his source of inspiration towards attaining a sense of self, he realizes that his perceptions of her are wrong. This realization provides him with a more optimistic outlook of life' (Sivapalan, 2007: 135).

THE PROBLEMATICS OF POSTCOLONIAL IDENTITY AND THE RELATIONSHIP BETWEEN PERSONAL AND SOCIAL DIMENSIONS AS WELL AS ISSUES THAT TRANSCEND BOTH DIMENSIONS: A CONCLUSION

The analysis shows 'that the postcolonial individual's identity is not permanent but is ever evolving. This constantly changing nature of the postcolonial individual's identity is a result of the individual's negotiation and repositioning of his identity in terms of personal and social perspectives. The individual's evolving identity can also be contributed to the fact that he has to negotiate between the identity developed in relation to his homeland culture and that which results from his confrontations with trans-cultural experiences' (Sivapalan, 2007: 135-136).

From the analysis, 'it was found that the protagonist has to negotiate changes to his identity and sense of self derived from his Malayan homeland with that which evolves as a result of transcultural confrontations in London. Although the protagonist regards Malaya as his homeland, he is not a native of the country. The protagonist's existence as a Malaysian can be traced back to the time his ancestors left China to start life anew in Malaya. As the protagonist was conceived in Malaya, he automatically becomes a Malaysian of immigrant Chinese descent. Being of immigrant Chinese descent, and staying in Malaysia, the protagonist must negotiate his identity and sense of self from two perspectives, i.e. his identity and sense of self as a Malaysian and as an immigrant Chinese. His positioning of identity and sense of self as a Malaysian is carried out through his cultural, racial, gender and sexual experiences in Malaya. His immigrant Chinese identity is seen at play through the beliefs and traditions of his Chinese culture which are embedded in his collective unconscious, possibly passed on to him by his parents and grandparents. The uncertain sense of self compels the protagonist to embark on a search for identity abroad. However, when he goes to London, he is confronted with similar problems. This makes him conclude that home is better off after all. The postcolonial individual's identity is repositioned through two stages. These stages are the majority identity development stage and the minority identity development stage. In the minority identity development stage, the postcolonial migrant individual goes through four levels of identity development. These levels are the unexamined identity, the period of conformity, resistance and separatism and integration. In the majority identity development stage, the postcolonial migrant individual's identity develops in five stages i.e. the level of unexamined identity, acceptance, resistance, redefinition and integration. In the novel, the protagonist experiences selected levels of the minority and majority identity development stages. The minority identity development levels experienced by the protagonist are the unexamined identity, conformity, resistance and separatism and integration. The protagonist's unexamined identity is revealed in his acceptance of the dominant norms of the host society. Conformity is seen when he assimilates the host culture. The protagonist does not totally embrace every cultural, racial, gender and sexual orientation of the home culture and does not reject all personal and social aspects of the host culture. Instead, he selects and invents from the materials of the home and host culture. At this point transcultural knowledge comes in handy for the protagonist. The protagonist then is able to identify himself with the culture of his homeland and the culture of the host country. This ability is known as transnationalism. The protagonist then is able to develop a secure identity and sense of self. This stage reflects his integration. In terms of majority identity development, the protagonist experiences the unexamined identity stage, the resistance stage, the redefinition stage and the integration stage. The protagonist's unexamined identity in the majority development stage is also revealed in his acceptance of the dominant customs of the host country. The resistance stage showcases his opposition to the ways in which cultural privilege is bestowed upon the members of the host society. In the stage of redefinition, the protagonist openly challenges these cultural privileges. In the stage of integration, the protagonist achieves a sense of belonging to the host culture and is also aware and appreciative of the values of his homeland culture. This stage indicates that the protagonist has developed a secure identity and sense of self. This developing nature of his identity and sense of self also affects the protagonist's formation of identity and sense of self from a postcolonial perspective. In the process of negotiating and forming his identity, the protagonist faces numerous experiences of marginalization, alienation, displacement and othering. It was also rather clear that these experiences made the protagonist view himself and the people around him in a different light. Although the protagonist was initially at a loss to who he was, he gradually began to comprehend his situation. This was done with the help of characters like Cordelia, Beatrice, Tristam and Guy. Towards the end of the novel, we find that the protagonist has finally come to terms with his identity and sense of self and is ready to return home. However, it must be highlighted that that process of repositioning the identity is an on-going one. Thus, the protagonist must once again re-evaluate his identity and sense of self as a result of his transcultural experiences upon his return to Malaya. This is because the Malaya he left may not be the same Malaya he will go back to. This redefinition of his identity enhances the notion that the identity is never a fixed entity' (Sivapalan, 2007: 136-138).

BIBLIOGRAPHY

Abdul Majid bin Nabi Baksh. 1984. Theme and technique in Lee Kok Liang's flower in the sky. *Southeast Asian Review of English*. **9**:16.

Abdul Rahman Embong. 1997. *National literatures in Malaysia towards a definition*. Bangi: Penerbit Universiti Kebangsaan Malaysia.

Abrams, M. H. 1999. *A glossary of literary terms*.7th Ed. New York: Holt, Reinhart and Winston.

Amuta, C. 1989. *A dialectical theory of African literature: categories and springboard: the theory of African literature*. London: Zed Books.

Ashcroft, B, Griffiths, G & Tiffin, H. 1989. *The empire writes back: theory and practice in post-colonial literatures.* London : Routledge.

Ashcroft, B, Griffiths, G, & Tiffin, H. 1998. *Key concepts in post-colonial studies*. London: Routledge.

Ashcroft, B & Ahluwalia, P. 2001. *Edward Said*. 2nd Ed. London: Routledge.

Ashmore, R. D. & Jussim, L. 1997. *Self and identity: fundamental issues*. Oxford: Oxford University Press.

Ban Kah Choon. 1998. Singapore/Malaysia fiction. (online) www.thecore.nus.edu/post/singapore/literature/fiction/fiction1.html (5th January 2004).

Barnes, J. 1985. The fiction of Lee Kok Liang. In: Mohammad A. Quayum & Peter C. Wicks (ed.). *Malaysian literature in english a critical reader.* pp. 184-190. Petaling Jaya: Pearson Education Malaysia.

Barry, P. 1995. *Beginning theory: an introduction to literary and cultural theory.* Manchester: Manchester University Press.

Baumeister, R. F. 1986. *Identity cultural change and the struggle for self.* New York: Oxford University Press.

Brown, J. A. C. 1961.*Freud and the post-Freudians.* Great Britain: Cox and Wyman Ltd.

Burke, P & Stets, J. 2000. Identity theory and social identity theory. *Social Psychology Quarterly.* **63** (3): 224-237.

Butcher, J. B. 1979. *The British in Malaya 1880-1941: the social history of a European community in South-East Asia.* Kuala Lumpur: Oxford University Press.

De Souza, D. 1984. The roots of Malay[an] literature in English. In: Mohd A Quayum & Peter Wicks (ed.). *Malaysian literature in English a critical reader,* pp. 2-12. Petaling Jaya: Pearson Education Malaysia Sdn Bhd.

Elliott, A. 1994. *Psychoanalytical theory an introduction.* Oxford: Blackwell Publishers.

Eriksen T. H. 2001. *Social identity, intergroup conflict, and conflict reduction.* Oxford: Oxford University Press.

Erikson, E. 1959. *Identity and life cycle.* New York: International Universities Press.

Erikson, E. 1968. *Identity, youth, and crisis.* New York: Norton.

Fadillah Merican, Ruzy Suliza Hashim, Ganakumaran Subramaniam & Raihanah Mohd. Mydin. 2004. *Voices of many worlds Malaysian literature in English.* Shah Alam: Times Editions.

Fanon, F. 1966. *The wretched of the earth.* New York: Grove Press Inc.

Fernando, L. 1986. *Cultures in conflict: essays on literature and the English language in South East Asia.* Singapore: Graham Brash (Pte) Ltd.

Fordham, F. 1966. *An Introduction to Jung's psychology.* (3rd Ed). Great Britain: The Chaucer Press Ltd.

Fordham, M. 1980. *Analytical psychology: a modern science.* London: Academic Press Inc.

Gilroy, P, Grossberg, L & McRobbie, A. 2000. *Without guarantees.* London: Verso.

Hall, S. 1986. Gramsci's relevance for the study of race and ethnicity. *Journal of communication inquiry* **10**: 5-27.

Hall, S. 1988. New ethnicities. *Black Film, British Cinema* **7**: 27-31.

Hall, S. 1991. Old and new identities. In: Anthony D. King (ed.). *Culture, globalization and the world-system: contemporary conditions for the representation of identity,* pp. 41-68. Binghamton: Macmillan.

Hall, S. 1998. Subjects in history: making diasporic identities. In: Wahneema Lubiano (ed.).*The House that Race Built,* pp. 289-300. New York: Vintage.

Han Suyin. 1966. *Anthology of modern Malaysian Chinese stories.* Singapore: Heinemann.

Harrex, S. C. 1979. Mutes and mutilators in the fiction of Lee Kok Liang. In: Daniel Massa (ed.). *Individual and community in commonwealth literature*, pp. 142. Malta: The University Press.

Harrex, S. C. 1982. Scalpel, scar, icon: Lee Kok Liang's 'Flowers in the Sky'. In: Mohammad A. Quayum & Peter C. Wicks (ed.). *Malaysian literature in English a critical reader*, pp 174-183. Petaling Jaya: Pearson Education Malaysia.

Harrex, S. C. 2003. Malaysian novel emerges from the past to take a critical look at England. (online) www.person.flinders.edu.au (19th December 2003).

Holaday, Woon-Ping Chin. 1988. Hybrid blooms: the emergent poetry in English of Malaysia and Singapore. In: C. Koelb and S. Noakes (ed.). *The Comparative Perspectives on Literature*, pp. 130-146. Ithaca: Cornell University Press.

James, William 1980. The principles of psychology. In: Peter Adler and Patricia A. Adler (ed.). *Symbolic Interactionism*, pp 20-61. Boston: Allyn and Bacon.

Jung, C. G. 1964. *Man and his symbols*. New York: Dell Publishing.

Jung, C G.1991. *The development of personality*. Great Britain: Routledge.

Kee Thuan Chye. 1992. *Just in so many words*. Singapore: Heinemann Asia.

Kirpal, V. 1988. *What is the modern third world novel?* **23** (1): 144-155.

Kirpal Singh. 1981. Flowers in the sky. *Singapore Book World* **12**: 46.

Kirpal Singh. 2000. Transcending context: the world of Lee Kok Liang's fiction. In: Mohammad A. Quayum & Peter C. Wicks (ed.). *Malaysian literature in English a critical reader*, pp. 204-211. Petaling Jaya: Pearson Education Malaysia.

Kwan-Terry, J. 1984. Narration and the structure of experience: the fiction of Lee Kok Liang. In: C. E. Nicholson & R. Chatterjee (ed.). *Tropic Crucible: Self and theory in language and literature*, pp. 143-162. Singapore: National University Press.

Lee Kok Liang. 2003. *London does not belong to me.* Petaling Jaya: Maya Press.

Lim Ai Lee. 1992. One of our best fiction writers. *New Straits Times,* 8th April: 34.

Lye, J. 1998. Psychoanalysis and literature.(online) http://www.brocku. ca/english/courses/4F70/postcol.html (30th December 2001).

Mak Lau Fong 1993. Occupation and Chinese dialect in British Malaya. In Leo Suryadinata (ed.). *Chinese adaptation and diversity: essays on society and literature in Indonesia, Malaysia and Singapore,* pp. 8-27. Singapore: Singapore University Press.

Maniam, K. S. 1987. The Malaysian novelist: detachment of spiritual transcendence. In: Mohammad A. Quayum & Peter C. Wicks (ed.). *Malaysian literature in English: a critical reader,* pp. 80-84. Petaling Jaya: Pearson Education Malaysia.

McClintok, A. 1995. *Imperial leather: race, gender, and sexuality in the colonial context.* New York: Routledge.

Mc Leod, A. L. 1966. *Malaysian literature in English. literature east and west.* **10**: 315-324.

Menninger, K A. 1979. *The human mind.* 20th Ed. United States: Alfred A. Knopf.

Mohammad A. Quayum & Wicks, P. 2001. *Malaysian literature in English: a critical reader.* Petaling Jaya: Pearson Education Malaysia.

Muhammad Hj. Salleh. 1998. Literature: the knowledge beyond. Working paper Commonwealth Writer's Seminar. Kuala Lumpur.

Munroe, R L.1955. *Schools of psychoanalytic thought*. New York: Holt, Rinehart and Winston.

Pratt, M. L.1992. *Imperial eyes: travel writing and transculturation*. London: Routledge.

Purcell, V. 1948. *The Chinese in Malaya*. London: Oxford University Press.

Roosens, Eugeen E. 1989. *Creating ethnicity*. London: Sage.

Rupprecht.1999. Archetypal theory and criticism. (online) http://www.press.jhu.edu/ooks/groden/free/archetypal_theory_and_criticism. html (15th December 2001).

Said, E. 1979. *Orientalism*. New York: Vintage.

Schultz, D. P. & Schultz S. E. 2001.*Theories of personality*.7th Ed. Belmont: Wadsworth.

Shweder, R. A. 1991. *Thinking through cultures*. Cambridge: Harvard University Press.

Smith, P., & Bond, M. H. 1999. *Social psychology across cultures*. 2nd Ed. Boston: Allyn and Bacon.

Sills, S. J. 2002. Transnationalizing the self: transitions in identity among marginalized labor migrants. (online) http://www.daneprairie.com (3rd January 2004).

Sivapalan, S. 2007. Transcultural experiences and the sense of self in London Does Not Belong To Me. In:Ruzy Suliza Hashim, Ismaznizam Azyze, Noraini Md. Yusof and Zalina Mohd Lazim (ed). Re-visioning realities through literary discourse: pp.125-138. Malaysia: Pearson.

Solehah Ishak 1987. *Histrionics of development: a study of three contemporary playwrights.* Kuala Lumpur: Dewan Bahasa dan Pustaka.

Subramaniam. G. 1996. Ethnocentricity in post-colonial Malaysian literary works: extent of unity in diversity. In: Fadillah Merican, Ruzy Suliza Hashim, Ganakumaran Subramaniam & Raihanah Mohd. Mydin. (ed.). *A View of Our Own: Ethnocentric Perspectives in Literature,* pp. 355-363. Malaysia: Universiti Kebangsaan Malaysia.

Subramaniam, G. 1996. Ideological stylistics: collative explorations in Malaysian and Singaporean fictional discourse. Ph.D Dissertation. University of Nottingham.

Tajfel, H. 1970. Experiments in intergroup discrimination. *Scientific American* 1: 96-102.

Tajfel, H. 1982 *Social identity and intergroup relations.* Cambridge: Cambridge University Press.

Tajfel, H. and Turner, J. C. 1986. The social identity theory of inter-group behavior. Chicago: Nelson-Hall.

Terry, S. 2000. *The Christian Science Monitor.* (online) http://www.csmonitor.com/durable/2000/08/28/fp1s4-csm.shtml (3rd January 2004)

Tham Seong Chee. 1981. The politics of literary development in Malaysia. In: Mohammad A. Quayum & Peter C. Wicks (ed.). *Malaysian literature in English: a critical reader,* pp. 80-84. Petaling Jaya: Pearson Education Malaysia.

Tyson, L. 1999. *Critical theory today a user friendly guide.* USA: Library of Congress.

Wallace, R & Wolf, A. 1980. *Contemporary sociological theory.* New Jersey: Prentice-Hall Inc.

Welsh, B.1996. Attitudes towards democracy in Malaysia: challenges to the regime: *Asian Survey* **9**: 882-903.

Wignesan, T. 1966. Literature in Malaysia. *The Journal of Commonwealth Literature* **2**: 113-123.

Williams, B. 1973. *Problems of the self.* Cambridge: Cambridge University Press.

Williams, P & Laura C. 1993.*Colonial discourse & postcolonial theory: a reader.* Harvester: Whaeatsheaf.

Wilson, B. 2003. Sketches, vignettes and brush strokes: portraits of the (Malaysian) writer as a young man. (online) http://social.chass.ncsu.edu/jouvert/v7i2/bwils.html (29th December 2003).

Wilson, B. 2003. Submerging pasts in London does not belong to me. Petaling Jaya: Maya Press.

Wong Phui Nam. 1992. A kind of Buddhist hell. *New Straits Times,* 5th August: 33.

Woods, S. 1990. Silence, communication and cultural conflict in Lee Kok Liang's 'The mutes in the sun' and 'Flowers in the sky'. In: Mohammad A. Quayum & Peter C. Wicks (ed.). *Malaysian literature in English a critical reader,* pp. 191-203. Petaling Jaya: Pearson Education Malaysia.

Zawiah Yahya. 1988. *Malay characters in Malaysian novels in English.* Monograph 1. Language Centre. Universiti Kebangsaan Malaysia.

Zawiah Yahya 1996. Literature in English and nation-building. *The Language Culture Connection.* RELC Anthology **37**: 9-16.